D1289600

AUTOMATIC TEACHING¦

The State of the Art

Edited by EUGENE GALANTER
University of Pennsylvania

with contributions by

Nancy S. Anderson
Jacob Beck
Robert C. Bolles
R. C. Brainerd
Leslie J. Briggs
Norman A. Crowder
Robert M. Gagne
Eugene Galanter
Robert Glaser
James G. Holland
Lloyd E. Homme
Howard H. Kendler
A. A. Lumsdaine
Susan R. Meyer
Douglas Porter
S. L. Pressey
Gustave J. Rath
B. F. Skinner
Donald E. P. Smith
David Zeaman

AUTOMATIC TEACHING:

The State of the Art

NEW YORK . JOHN WILEY & SONS, INC.

London . Chapman & Hall, Limited

Copyright © 1959
BY
John Wiley & Sons, Inc.

All Rights Reserved

*This book or any part thereof must not
be reproduced in any form without
the written permission of the publisher.*

Library of Congress Catalog Card Number: 59-14118

PRINTED IN THE UNITED STATES OF AMERICA

LB1029
.A85
.G3

INTRODUCTORY REMARKS

On December 8 and 9, 1958 the University of Pennsylvania and the Air Force Office of Scientific Research were hosts for a first conference on the Art and Science of the Automatic Teaching of Verbal and Symbolic Skills. * This report presents several of the papers and abstracts that were read at the meeting, and a related paper by Gagné and Bolles.

As a technique, teaching by machine is quite new; as an object of experimental study it dates at least from Pressey's early papers. The total accumulated empirical information, although large, is scattered, and its analysis and reduction is fraught with difficulty. For this reason most of the papers in this volume generate more problems than they illuminate. These proceedings are published, not to provide information for the implementation of school or military curricula by machine instruction, but to aid the researcher in isolating parameters for study and to provide him with the currently available information in this field. It is to be expected that as reliable results from field tests and laboratory studies are published these papers will be outdated. It is further to be hoped that the speculations that are made in this report will be validated or rejected in as short a time as possible.

We acknowledge with thanks the help provided to us by Mr. Paul Dittman, representative of the Air Force Office of Scientific Research, and Vice-Provost

*This conference was supported in part by the Air Force Office of Scientific Research under Contract AF 49(638)-187.

v

Sculley Bradley of the University of Pennsylvania; by Mrs. Jane Levine, who singlehandedly accomplished all the organizational details for the conference; by Mrs. Phyllis Ellis for her adroit work on the manuscript; and especially we acknowledge the help of the Hughes Aircraft Company for their invaluable aid in the composition of this report.

Galanter
Center for Advanced Study in the
Behavioral Sciences

May, 1959

TABLE OF CONTENTS

1

Eugene Galanter
University of Pennyslvania

THE IDEAL TEACHER

The development of a successful machine that will teach a person the complex of interlocking symbolic and verbal knowledge that is the mark of an education is equivalent to a general theory of learning and teaching. This is quite a prize for the psychologist, and the practical and technological ramifications are both obvious and perhaps a trifle terrifying. After all, a machine that can do this job is, by definition, a good teacher, and good teachers since the beginnings of recorded history have been considered quite humane humans. A humane machine seems to most laymen either a laughable contradiction, or the final depravity of the scientific mind. Many of the papers in this volume constitute rebuttals to this concern. The general form that the arguments take is that the machines are <u>merely</u> <u>aids</u> to teaching. They are the elaborate toys of psychological technology. In fact they are criticized by some as not incorporating the findings of psychological theory, and therefore are ripe for improvement by the application of principles that have been found in standard psychological experimentation.

Our thesis is quite the opposite. These machines, when they work, are a theory of teaching. Research to improve upon and to expand the theory must take the structure of the machine into account. The study of teaching machine effectiveness is not, to us, an exercise

1

in applied psychology. Rather, it is an experimental technique for the exploration of fundamental problems in the psychology of the higher mental processes. To say that a machine is a theory may run counter to the scientific attitude that many of us express. But there is an important sense in which this must be true. The initial state of any machine is describable in a finite language. The mechanism that transforms the machine from state to state can be expressed as a set of operations on the language that describes the initial state; therefore subsequent states of the machine can be derived from the initial state by the rules of transformation. These last sentences comprise the characterization of a theory. Any self-modifying process with a large number of potential transition states (that is, a process whose transitions are invented to respond to a potentially infinite set of inputs) is difficult to express in a simple notation. Therefore a good teaching machine and its evolving pattern cannot be described in detail, it must be displayed.

What would a machine like this look like? That is, what would constitute its internal constraints? If we knew the answer to this question the problem would be solved. But even if a complete answer is not feasible, perhaps we can reach some agreement about the functions it would have to perform, and from a consideration of these functions find the explicit and particular problems that empirical research can illuminate.

Stated another way, can we delimit the kinds of operations that an optimum teacher must perform? Let us hasten to add that these questions are not designed to suggest that we abandon work on simple devices for teaching; this is a task to which most of our energies must be directed. The remarks in this paper refer to a, perhaps unrealizable, ideal teaching device. But some of the features of the device may be captured in the simpler methods that will undoubtedly remain our stock-in-trade.

The nature of an optimum teaching machine may best be revealed by considering the questions that many members of this conference found to be of importance.

Many of the papers in this conference are concerned with these particular problems:

1. The programming problem--what is the correct order of presentation of material?

2. The error rate problem--is there an optimum number of errors that should be made?

3. The step size problem--How far apart (in some sense) should adjacent items of the program be spaced?

4. The prompting problem--should prompts be used, and if so how and what kind?

5. The constructive vs. multiple choice response problems.

6. The pacing problem--experimenter-controlled rate vs. self-pacing.

7. The multiple track problem--is one program satisfactory for all students?

8. The economic problem--how much is additional education worth?

9. The generalization or testing problem--how do you know that the student has learned?

We shall argue that a machine that will cope
with these problems must have certain features imposed
upon its design. In particular the machine must be able
to respond to the student, and to receive from him certain kinds of information. All current machines have
this feature. But additionally, we shall point out that an
optimum machine should be able to make plans for itself,
and also be able to diagnose the plans and ideas that the
student has formed.

When we say that a machine must make plans,
we mean simply that it must be able to guide its own
behavior; that it can absorb information from the student,
and on the basis of the information, form for itself a
scheme for presenting its own ideas to the student. The
machine's actions that are guided by the plan must be
evaluated, and it must be capable of changing its plans
in the light of new input information; i. e. , it must not be
rigid. A general description of plans and their role in
psychology can be found in (1).

In current teaching machine technology the plan
of the machine, usually called its program, has been
placed in the hands of the human designer. Our aim shall
be to reduce this component of the machine's plan to a
minimum. The result we anticipate is that when we
understand how the machine's plans are formed, the
problems that have been posed will evaporate. Evaporate, of course, only in principle; but hopefully our
results will serve as a plan to guide us in our experimentation so that the problems will in fact dissolve with
a minimum of empirical flailing.

Implicit in our previous remarks is the notion
that the ideal teacher for a given student depends on the
student. This is true only if the differences between
students are large enough to make alternative programs
economically feasible. To answer this question we must

reach some common understanding as to what constitutes an alternative program. Let us suppose that we have broken some subject matter down into its minimal elements. Forego for the moment what these elements are or how they are to be characterized. Suppose also that each element requires one of two mutually exclusive and exhaustive responses by the student, and that for each of these responses, the teacher selects the next element, with an eye to which response was made. This is essentially Crowder's scrambled book (see Chapter X). The number of possible paths through the subject matter will then be 2^n if there are n elements. Add to this the number of programs that involve potential deletions, given that a student is progressing with zero error, and the number of programs is enormous. Clearly, most of these programs are irrelevant because we already have some strong intuitions about sensible orders of elements, but if we allow recursions that retrace past elements in the case of numerous errors, we still have a lot of programs. What then does one do to reduce this infinity of possible programs to a small subset, and still preserve some respect for the students' capabilities? Skinner has already considered one solution; the program order is fixed, but recursions to previously failed elements occur. An additional flexibility can be achieved by allowing dropouts or item deletions in the program. Thus the better student can skip ahead.

Now these two techniques for tailoring programs to the students depend on the machine's knowing whether the student should be returned to an earlier part of the program or moved ahead. The only information that will serve this purpose is the error probability. Therefore, the question of error rate takes on a new look. Errors are important, even for Professor Skinner, because they are the signals that the machine uses to modify its own actions. When error has a high probability, the machine should return to earlier material.

When the error probability is too small, the machine
should drop out items and move ahead. The error probability should then tend to hover around some optimum
value. What value? That becomes the important empirical question. We suspect that for verbal or symbolic
material (what we call digital material) the error probability should be quite low; perhaps less than 10%. Here
we are in agreement with the Harvard group. For skilled
action training (analogue material) like motor tracking,
or writing, error probability should, we think, be somewhat higher; perhaps 15 to 20%.

Suppose then that the machine can backtrack to
earlier material or speed up to later material depending
on the error rate, should it advance or retard to the same
elements every time? The problem seems to be critical
for finding minimal programs. Perhaps backtracking
should lead to "new" old elements, or perhaps to the old
elements with additional prompts. Some study of prompting before and after errors would throw some useful
light on this issue. Before we leave this topic we should
comment on one point that seems to have been confused
in some of the discussion. It was frequently asserted
that "errors" helped the student to form sharper dis-
criminations, and therefore that fairly high error prob-
abilities were useful. This seems odd. Certainly what
proponents of this view probably meant was that the
student should be required to detect an inaccurate or
inappropriate item; that he should learn to say, "No,
that's the wrong way to state Ohm's Law." But the de-
tection of errors is not the commission of errors. We
see no reason to suppose that a program that aids in the
commission of errors can be valuable. Errors that the
student makes only serve to provide information to the
teacher. We need the information, but not the errors.
We retain some errors only because we believe that
different students require different programs, and the
errors serve as an economical signal. When the student

makes an error the machine reads it as, "I don't understand; do something to help me. "

If we have a set of atomic items for a program,
then as we have suggested above, deletion of items contingent on low error probability sets the inter-item step
size, and this problem vanishes to become a special
feature of machine design, not program design. A general program is one that contains the exhaustive set of
atomic items. Now although we have sidestepped the
step-size problem we have introduced another, and
probably more difficult problem.

An exhaustive set of atomic items for, say, an
arithmetic program contains an example of every problem in arithmetic. This set is clearly infinite. But we
do not want such a complete set, because we believe
that the person is not really learning to solve every separate arithmetic problem, S-R learning theory to the
contrary notwithstanding. Rather, we hope that the student is learning a scheme or plan for solving any problem, a plan that can be extracted from a rather small
set of examples. So the step-size problem changes into
the sampling problem of the universe of possible atomic
items. This, of course, is the concept identification
chestnut. And what teaching machine theory suggests is
that we find teaching machines that will produce concepts.
In the standard form of concept identification, the subject is required to read the experimenter's mind. The
question that is asked is how long does it take? Sometimes, if the experimenter is sophisticated, he may also
ask how the concept was found. But from our side of the
fence this is a thankless problem. We must discover
ways to produce the formation of concepts, not tricks to
slow it down. The experiment is no longer one in which
the subject matches wits with the experimenter. Our
task is to find that sequence of items from the universe
of the concept that will effectively produce the concept in

the mind of the student. We have an essentially infinite
universe of examples; how should the universe be sam-
pled Well, it probably depends on whether we know
how to generate the universe of items or not. For arithmetic there exists an algorithm that tells you how to
produce every problem in the arithmetic of the integers.
You might very well sample items by programming a
computer to spin out the items and then select according
to some random sampling scheme. But usually there
will be no algorithm that will tell you what the items are.
In that case you must adopt some heuristic device to
generate items, and then sample from them in terms of
some set of rules. Our ideal teacher then, would digest
the available literature in an area, devise a heuristic for
generating items, and then sample according to some
plan or other.

We have spoken so far as though the teacher
will accept only multiple choice inputs. This seems
simply to beg the question of constructive vs. multiple
choice responses. But really we do not beg the issue;
we simply decide it. For verbal materials, the nature
of the response is digital. That is, the response does
not "look like" or have "a magnitude equivalent to" the
notion that is expressed. Rather, it is a symbol or mark
that has been decided arbitrarily to "stand for" the idea,
as a printed digit "stands for" a certain quantity. In this
sense all verbal teaching is digital and therefore multiple
choice. The response may, however, be composed of a
string or sequence of digital elements (cf. Chapter XI)
In that case it would be called "constructive, " but it is
still multiple choice. Only the choice set has been en-
larged. This question then is one of how large the choice
set should be, and whether we want to teach people to
generate the elements of choice. A valuable problem to
work on, we think. For the training of certain motor
skills, of course, the response is not, and indeed cannot
be digital. But in this area, training devices have

achieved a certain success, and perhaps we had better
leave this problem to the gentlemen (women) better able
to handle it.

     The problem of testing the student has two facets
for our ideal machine. On the one hand certain items
are "test" items even though they are inherent in the
program. They require responses for which the cues
within the item are minimal. This is a point that Beck
makes in Chapter III.. In addition, it may be wise to include items for which the answer or reinforcement is
not immediately given to the student. That is, we may
want to introduce a partial reinforcement schedule. How
the schedule can be introduced, and whether it has the
effects that we have observed in other experiments, is a
topic that will certainly be investigated. A reasonable
conjecture is that an extending aperiodic schedule may
enhance the inherent interest in the subject matter, as it
seems to do in animal experiments. As far as "testing
the limits" by measuring generalization is concerned,
there is no doubt that Kendler is right (see Chapter XV),
but certainly our machine can and must produce items
that make such tests.

     What now about speed? So far we have con-
sidered the teacher as subject-controlled. But we do
not really expect to allow the student an indefinite time
to answer each question. Should there be a time-out
mechanism? Should the machine say, after a longish
wait for an answer, "You really must do something, old
boy, I can't wait forever." Probably so, in fact, an
important element in many verbal skills is a certain
speed of performance. Time pressure, introduced
gradually, would seem to be a valuable addition to the
machine's design. Certainly a completely machine-
paced approach; as in educational TV or movies, seems
wasteful. The timing may very well depend on the machine's taking in time information from the student;

that is, computing an average time to answer, and then
pushing that time back slowly. This seems a likely candidate for the solution of the pacing problem.

What if the "constitutionalists" are right, and
in fact some people could never learn to solve differential equations? Our machine has no stop order, so its
plan will continue to be executed until the machine or the
student wears out. With recycling to earlier segments
as an intrinsic part of its design the teacher could go on
forever. Is this economically or educationally feasible?
Clearly not. Some kind of test for stopping must be introduced into the machine's plan so that the instruction
can be terminated without too much waste. Again error
probability seems the likely candidate as a signal, with
a little modulation by the number of cycles that the student has needed in the recent past. The trick is to stop
the student after the machine is sure that continuing will
do no more good, but not before. This cut-off problem
is better left to society to determine. We can only suggest the kinds of criteria that might be acceptable.

We have saved the hardest problem until the
end, possibly with the hope that the reader would be
tired by this time, and therefore less critical of the
confusions in the plan of the author. This problem is,
quite naturally, the programming problem. Can we
think of a mechanism that will program or order the
atomic elements of the material to be learned? A trivial
solution is to have the machine number the items arbitrarily, and then select item 1 from its memory and
present it to the student; if he should fail, it selects
item 2 after moving the first to the end of the list of
candidates, while if the student is successful it goes on.
If the student or the machine doesn't quit in disgust, this
scheme is sure to work. After the final exposure, the
machine will have a program for this student. It might
even be a good program for all students. But it is the

hard way to do it. If the machine had some reasonable guesses to make about the difficulty of items, it might then arrange its selecting and ordering scheme with a bit more intelligence. The problem is to find a structural feature of items that gives an estimate of difficulty. Not an easy problem to solve, but some of the work of the computer engineers on self-programming machines may be relevant. This is not the place to enlarge on these topics, except to suggest that if we made known our problems to some of the computer people, we might get some interesting ideas.

We have trudged a long track, but perhaps it will make the retracing easier. As you look ahead into the more solid contributions in the following chapters, new ideas may come to you about how some of these difficult theoretical, empirical, and practical problems can be better formulated or solved. If this happens even to the minutest degree, then this machine has completed its program.

References

1. Miller, G. A. , E. Galanter and K. Pribram, Plans and the Structure of Behavior. (In Press)

2

Robert M. Gagné
Princeton University

Robert C. Bolles
University of Pennsylvania

A REVIEW OF FACTORS
IN LEARNING EFFICIENCY

From the very great amount of research that has been done on human learning much is known about the conditions that influence learning, and many of the variables that govern learning have now been identified. It is somewhat surprising that in spite of this body of information, relatively little of a systematic nature is known about how to promote efficient learning in practical situations.

There are probably several reasons for this discrepancy. First, much of the experimental research has been directed toward testing theoretical points which have little immediate practical application. The researcher typically is concerned with understanding how the learning process functions, and not with the question of how to implement learning.

Second, laboratory studies frequently demonstrate the effect of some variable influencing learning by providing conditions that lead to a decrement in performance. It is not altogether obvious that the conditions that facilitate learning can be safely inferred from such studies.

Experimental studies of learning have tended to involve rather restricted stimulus material far removed from the kinds of material that are of importance practically. The learning tasks that have been most intensively studied by psychologists have been of an artificial

13

"laboratory" variety; relatively little is known about learning in real life situations. On the other hand, educators, who do work with practical learning situations, have not done the systematic, controlled type of study that is needed to reveal general principles of learning efficiency.

Finally, the criterion of learning employed in most laboratory studies of learning almost always is confined to performance in the learning situation. More pertinent for the purposes of the Air Force would be a criterion involving subsequent performance in a job situation.

For all of these reasons, there appears to be a gap between what is known about learning in the laboratory and learning in the training-job situation. The purpose of this report is to describe and evaluate the findings which might contribute to bridging this gap. Before treating this material directly, we must first discuss several general problems in order to delimit the scope of this report. These problems are: (1) establishing the most useful criteria of learning efficiency; (2) selecting the kinds of tasks for which principles of learning efficiency are to be sought; and (3) a specification of the "structure" of learning, by which is meant a classification of the factors that influence learning efficiency.

The main body of this report deals with principles derived from laboratory findings and theoretical writings that seem relevant to the problem of promoting efficient learning. In describing these factors and their origin, we have not attempted to provide a detailed review containing all relevant references. Instead, reference is usually made to a key paper, set of studies, or to an authoritative work summarizing the field. Consideration is given to the kind of evidence which exists, the suggestions it has for learning efficiency, and its adequacy

in dealing with this problem. Following this review some
conclusions are drawn regarding the present state of
knowledge of these principles and the research questions
which appear to be in need of investigation.

Criteria of Learning Efficiency

In seeking to understand the learning process,
the psychologist who studies learning typically confines
his investigation to a single situation, that in which the
learning occurs. He is not usually concerned with what
the effects of training in another situation will be. Thus,
it is quite natural for him to use, as a criterion of learning efficiency, the number of trials required to produce
some arbitrary standard of performance on the learning
task.

But the Air Force is concerned with training a
man in one situation to perform on the job in a somewhat
different situation. Performance in the initial learning
or training situation is of lesser practical importance
than the degree of transfer that can be effected to the job
situation. The purpose of training is thus to equip the
trainee with the ability to perform adequately in a situation that is novel in some respect. Consequently, the
present report will primarily emphasize transfer rather
than learning per se. In other words, the measure of
learning effectiveness we will deal with most frequently
is amount of transfer.

There still remains some question regarding
the criterion of efficiency. One could refer to a learning
or training program as being efficient if it required only
a short training period, or if it were inexpensive, or if
it were successful with a high proportion of the trainees.
While each of these possible criteria has merit and may
be of primary consideration for some particular purpose,

we shall establish for the purpose of this report the following criterion of learning efficiency: <u>Learning will be</u>
<u>said to be efficient if it leads to a high level of perform-</u>
<u>ance in the transfer situation.</u> In accordance with this
view, considerations like amount of training are variables
which may have an influence on learning efficiency, but
they are not measures of it.

One further consideration is that sometimes a
training program is desired which will instruct the
trainee in a very specific task, one that never or rarely
changes. Efficiency of such a training program then
would be simply the proficiency at the given task and
would be just the specific transfer from training to that
task. But more frequently a training program is desired
which will instruct the trainee to perform a variety of
tasks, or equip him to shift readily from one task to
another, or even from one job to another. In this case
learning efficiency is given by the generalization or
broadness of transfer to a variety of tasks. Such training programs might well be anticipated to be more difficult to devise than ones from which only specific transfer
is required.

Kinds of Tasks

The conditions of learning efficiency are undoubtedly different for different tasks. If this is the case,
then we should not expect a general answer to the question of learning efficiency, applicable to the performance
involved in motor skills, procedure following, perceptual
skills, and problem solving. Each of these types of task
has its own peculiar conditions for learning efficiency.

Some of these tasks have widespread importance; others have a more limited importance. Accordingly, it seems worthwhile to set a limitation to the scope

of this report by emphasizing the learning of certain
types of tasks. In the following paragraph we shall discuss reasons for believing that identification, following
procedures, and concept using are types of tasks which
deserve emphasis for the problem of learning efficiency,
whereas motor skills constitute a less promising topic
at the present time. This particular classification of
types of tasks is not conceived as having a validity
greater than other possible categorizations. But it provides a convenient framework for the consideration of a
great variety of military jobs.

Identification. In psychological terms, identification learning means the acquisition of several different responses to the same number of different situations
or objects. The typical situation for the occurrence of
identification behavior is one in which a number of objects, events, or places must be identified by differen-
tiating names or other responses. The learning of identifications is one of the most common things a human
being does, from early childhood throughout his adult
life. Although this type of learning is common to nearly
all jobs, its importance can easily be overlooked. For
example, if a new job requires that an individual identify
only seven tools, we are inclined not to notice the fact
that he must learn these identifications, since the period
required for such learning is short. On the other hand,
many jobs require identification of hundreds of faces,
places, tools, or materials, and in such instances the
period of learning, or training, becomes an essential
requirement.

In the military services, with their frequently
changing jobs or parts of jobs occasioned by the introduction of new weapons, the learning of new sets of
identifications is a ubiquitous phenomenon. The pilot
who learns to operate a new aircraft must first learn to
identify the controls and instruments of the new cockpit.

The observer has to learn to identify targets from radar returns. The electronic technician who is being trained to maintain a new guidance system must first master the identification of its parts and their locations, as well as their symbols on schematic diagrams. The supply man who is most highly skilled is the one who can identify perhaps thousands of components and parts, and their bin locations, without going through the laborious process of tracing them down by nomenclature through a succession of technical orders. A particular sub-category of identification occurs in those instances in which the stimulus situation may be ordered on a physical dimension. Such is the case, for example, with the identification of distances, as performed by the pilot in landing a plane.

Following procedures. This kind of task is also relatively common among Air Force jobs. It is found, for example, in the procedures of "preflighting" an aircraft, preparing a radio set for operation, setting up a piece of test equipment, filling out forms. Individuals with a great deal of experience often amaze us by displaying the ability to carry out complex and long procedures without "looking them up" or referring to check lists.

Although the reinstatement of long procedures by memory is undoubtedly an efficient process, for most people such a task is accomplished by referring to lists of some sort. In such instances, since the sequence does not have to be retained, the task reduces to one of identification of the individual items of the procedure. Thus if an individual has a check-list saying: 1. Turn on Power Switch; 2. Set dial X to O; etc., the things to be learned are the identifications of "Power switch," "dial X," and so on, rather than the sequence of these items.

Tasks involving recalled procedures of medium

length may be of considerable importance to Air Force
jobs. Many of the procedures the pilot follows in the air
have to be done with a timing and promptness which will
not allow for "looking them up in the manual." Similarly,
many of the equipment-checking procedures of the maintenance man are most efficiently carried out by means of
retained sequences.

Concept using. Concepts are used in a variety
of Air Force jobs having certain formal characteristics
in common. They are used in numerical calculation, as
it occurs in many jobs including those of the pilot, navi-
gator, and maintenance technician. They are used to
guide behavior by means of rules, such as "always put
the account number in the upper right-hand corner," or
"turn power off before opening cover." And more im-
portantly, they are used in eliciting new responses by
generalization, in situations that partake of problem
solving. A number of critical Air Force jobs require
problem solving; included among them are aerial photo-
interpretation, equipment trouble-shooting, control of
aircraft tactics, interpretation of defense situations from
radar returns, and many others pertaining to the conduct
of aerial operations and logistics.

Somewhat in contrast to other tasks, it is generally recognized that these "concept-using" tasks cannot
be mastered simply by direct practice. Instead, something must be learned which mediates the performances
of calculation or problem solving, and this something is
concepts. So the problem of efficiency becomes one of
the efficient learning of useful concepts, by which is
meant those concepts that transfer to the performance
of the task.

Motor skills. The increasing use of automatic
equipment has tended to decrease progressively the pre-
valence of motor skills in Air Force jobs. The aircraft

is now flown by instruments rather than by the "seat
of the pants. " The tracking of targets is done by
radar. Automatically-controlled aerial gunnery has replaced "flexible" gunnery. In each of these instances,
and there are others which could be mentioned, a job
which originally required a motor skill has been
replaced by one which does not. Tool-using skills are
still required in maintenance (soldering, tightening,
etc.) but even these are being replaced or reduced to
a level of great simplicity by the introduction of
simple fasteners, plug-in circuits, and the like. Any
objective view of the matter must conclude that tasks
requiring motor skills are of diminishing importance
in the modern Air Force.

Implications for the scope of this report.
Our review of Air Force tasks for which learning
efficiency may be an important problem has considered
the occurrence of identification, following procedures,
concept-using and motor skills. From the standpoint
of importance and frequency of occurrence particularly, we are led to the conclusion that the first three
of these types of tasks should be emphasized in
consideration of the principles of learning efficiency.
In particular, identification and concept-using both
occur frequently in a great variety of jobs. Procedure-
following is of somewhat lesser significance, but
should not be overlooked. Motor skills appear to be
of decreasing importance in Air Force jobs.

Accordingly, subsequent sections of this
report will pay closest attention to the sources of
evidence pertaining to learning efficiency pointing to
performance of identification, procedural, and concept-
using tasks. We shall have occasion to refer, however, to studies of motor skills whenever these are
relevant to our main purpose.

The Manipulable Conditions of the Learning Situation

Efficiency of learning clearly depends upon 1) the individual who does the learning, 2) the nature of the task to be learned, and 3) the conditions under which the particular learning occurs. This report will not deal directly with the first two of these three broad categories, although we may note that work proficiency may be greatly enhanced by properly defining the job, and by assigning the proper man to do it. We shall restrict our discussion to the ways in which the learning or training situation itself can be manipulated to produce maximum transfer to the job situation.

In following this aim, we must exclude from consideration in this report the important matter of the trainee's general attitude toward the training program. If the trainee is not willing to submit to the learning situation, then he is not apt to learn much; there can hardly be any effective training possible for him.

Among the conditions of training situations which influence learning and which are accessible, that is, which are manipulable by those in charge of training programs, we may distinguish two classes. First, there are the motivational or preparatory conditions that make the trainee ready for learning.. We shall call these readiness factors. These include factors ranging from the general level of motivation to very specific sets to associate particular responses with particular stimuli. Second, there are a number of stimulus conditions to determine which specific associations are formed, and how strong these associations are relative to competing associations. These we call associative factors. Various degrees of importance are assigned by different writers to motivational and associative factors. But the evidence indicates that both are important, and while they interact

in virtually all learning situations, the present analysis
is considerably clarified by treating them separately.

Readiness factors. Most theorists seem to
agree that in learning to perform some task the individual
must actively seek some goal or incentive. The individual must be motivated (that is, he must try) to attain
some desirable consequence of his performance. Whether
this motivation-goal sequence is a necessary condition
for learning itself is a much debated theoretical issue;
but there is little doubt regarding the efficacy of motivation in producing overt performance.

Allied with conditions of motivation are the
conditions of reinforcement, or, put another way, the
conditions which govern how goals are actually attained.
The effects of reinforcement or goal attainment are
complicated; they serve not only to confirm the subject's
preceding behavior, but also to maintain the motivational
level. Further complications are introduced by the fact
that we are interested here primarily in transfer rather
than in original learning. Relatively little is known
about the role of motivational variables in transfer.

Another important readiness factor in the learning situation is what the learning subject is doing or
trying to do. This factor is generally called the subject's
task set. In general, it can be said that the learner will
do better if he knows what he's supposed to do. Task
set may be quite general, involving only knowledge of
what the completed task is like, or it may be quite specific, as when the person gets ready to press a key at a
given signal.

Associative factors. A second broad class of
variables comprises associative factors. These are the
stimulus conditions that enter into the learning situation
because they are the ones with which specific responses

are to be associated. According to one somewhat over-
simplified picture, the problem of controlling behavior
consists simply in strengthening association between
some stimulus and the desired response to the point
where the response will automatically occur whenever
the stimulus is presented. While we recognize the possibility of this simple kind of mediation we believe it is
practicable and useful to take advantage of other possible
types of mediation. Thus, we want to consider seriously
the efficiency of learning situations in which the desired
responses are associated with a variety of stimuli, and
are also mediated by the verbal or voluntary processes
of the trainee. This diversification of mediation would
seem to be especially useful in highly conceptual types
of tasks, as well as those in which variable rather than
fixed behavior is called for. Accordingly, we shall discuss later in the report principles which relate efficiency
of learning to the nature of what is learned. It seems
likely that, for some kinds of tasks, it is more important
that the trainee "understand the general principles"
underlying his work than that he know only something
specific about any particular piece of work. Such a
training program would call for the acquisition of a
mediating process probably not best characterized as a
stimulus-response association.

It is well known that if the training task is similar to the job situation then transfer to a final task (of
the job) will be directly related to the degree of learning
that occurs in the training task. However, to the extent
that the training task differs from the job situation, initial learning or overlearning will reduce the amount of
transfer and thus be inefficient. The precise degree of
similarity which determines the transition point, that is,
which determines how much learning is most effective,
is the crucial parameter here, but one about which we
know little. In any particular instance it is an empirical
question just how much learning will lead to the most

effective transfer. The reason for this practical limitation is that no well-accepted method is available which
makes possible the independent measurement of task
similarity. In fact, at the present stage of our knowledge
we sometimes depend upon the amount of transfer as an
index of similarity. Nonetheless, it is generally accepted
that in any specific application transfer is improved by
increasing similarity.

In the discussion which follows we have distinguished two roles played by both readiness and associative
factors. We conceive both to play a part in determining
the similarity between training task and job, and both to
be involved in determining the extent of initial learning
during the training period. Thus, we think of the ideal
training schedule as a two stage affair in which, first,
learning of the training task is optimized, and second,
transfer is insured by making the training task maximally
similar to that of the job situation.

Readiness Factors

Motivation

The place of motivational concepts in behavior
theory is ambiguous. Recently some writers have suggested that introducing these concepts into the explanation of behavior contributes little toward its explanation
(2, 24). These writers suggest that behavior may best
be accounted for in terms of detailed descriptions of the
conditions under which it is controlled. On the other
hand, we have inherited through the years a good deal of
evidence from social mores, from casual observation,
as well as from psychological laboratories, testifying to
the efficacy of controlling behavior by means of controlling what we call motivational variables. Thus, if we
seek to produce some particular kind of behavior in a
person, we should see to it that the person wants to

behave in that way.

Such a broad motivational rule would seem to be trivially obvious and beyond question. Probably there is nothing wrong with it as a general principle. Its fault lies in being too non-specific and too general; it tells us nothing about how to proceed in any given instance. Theoretical psychologists as well as those interested in applied problems are concerned with controlling and predicting behavior under specific circumstances. Hence, it is necessary to abandon the general rule and to seek in any given situation those particular conditions that maximize performance. To the extent that it is possible to describe kinds of non-associative conditions that contribute to performance, motivational concepts are useful.

We turn now to the question of how to regulate motivational variables in a training situation so as to maximize performance in that situation. On this question there is a good deal of relevant evidence. The classical finding is that performance improves as motivation increases (30, p. 413 ff.). Thus the most effective training program would be expected to be one for which motivation is maximal. This is probably true provided certain conditions are met. Spence and his co-workers have recently emphasized that before motivation can facilitate performance it is necessary that the correct or otherwise desired behavior be dominant over other possible behavior patterns (40). Thus, if the trainee's strongest or most probable response is not the desired one, increased motivation will lead to interference and to performance decrement. This follows from Spence's assumption that the effect of motivation is to facilitate indiscriminately any and all behavior which may be going on. Thus, for motivation to lead to superior performance, the responses which are required must be the ones which are dominant in a situation. If this view is correct (and it is still open to some question) it would suggest that the

most efficient learning procedure would be one in which
the level of motivation increases in the course of training so as to parallel the probability of the desired behavior. The efficacy of such a procedure has not yet
been tested experimentally, however.

Intrinsic vs. extrinsic motivation. Another
proviso to the general rule that motivation facilitates
performance is that the motivation should be, in some
sense, relevant to the task. There are a number of task
goals for which humans can be motivated. The task itself often provides some intrinsic motivation; the material
to be learned may be interesting in itself. Task completion often serves as a goal; other things being equal,
people desire to complete tasks they have started. The
value of task completion is further enhanced if the task
is one in which the trainee is ego-involved, so that pride
in success at the task becomes a goal. Desire to succeed
appears, in fact, to be a highly dependable source of
motivation for the learning situation.

By contrast with these sorts of goals there are
extrinsic goals. Success in the task at hand may serve
as a goal if the trainee is motivated to excel his fellows,
to compete with them. Another kind of extrinsic motivation which may be applicable in some situations is the
desire to please one's superiors. Still another is the
fondness for gambling. The tendency of people to like to
gamble is as yet a relatively unexploited possibility in
the design of teaching machines (39). Some other kinds
of extrinsic motivation approach irrelevance. For example, the learner may be motivated by anxiety over
possible failure, or over his inability to do as well as
his fellow trainees.

During most of the course of learning it is
probably important that motivation be relevant, and preferably that it be intrinsic. Once learning has proceeded

to a certain level of proficiency, so that the desired
behavior is dominant, it may be that the nature of motivation makes little difference; any source of motivation
may sustain performance. In any case, the idea that
motivation should be intrinsic rests not so much upon
the role motivation plays in learning or in performance
during learning; rather, it reflects a concern with the
transfer criterion. It seems reasonable to suppose that
motives and goals intrinsic to the task are more likely to
transfer to the job situation. One reason why training
performance is frequently an unreliable indication of
subsequent job proficiency may be that the trainee's
motives so often change between the transfer and the job
situations.

It should be emphasized that most of this discussion is necessarily speculative. To our knowledge,
nothing has been done experimentally to demonstrate
that motivation during the training has anything to do with
the degree of transfer to subsequent on-the-job performance. Furthermore, it seems likely that, even if a
systematic experimental research program should indicate the nature of the relationship between motivation
and transfer, it would still be necessary to determine
empirically what practical measures are required to
maximize transfer in any given application. Motivational
variables are perhaps the most exclusive concepts with
which psychologists work.

Levels of aspiration. Related to the factor of
motivation to succeed is the concept of "level of aspiration." The difference between the performance an individual thinks he can do, and what he actually accomplishes,
has been found to be an important motivational variable
(23). Thus, it turns out, that if the person's goal is set
too high he may become disappointed at his relative
failure to improve subsequently. On the other hand if
his goal is set too low that his learnings will not proceed,

he will not improve in the task. It is clear that there is
an optimum difference between the goal and the trainee's
level of aspiration. While this parameter is undoubtedly
an important one in learning, or at least in performance
during learning, its relationship to subsequent performance in a transfer situation remains an unexplored
problem.

Reinforcement

The problem of motivation and the problem of
reinforcement are highly interrelated. Generally, when
we know what a person's motive is, we also know how we
can reinforce his behavior. When motivation is intrinsic,
that is, when it depends in some way upon the nature of
the task, relevant reinforcement is provided by giving
the learner "knowledge of results." This is a type of
motivation-reinforcement sequence that has been studied
experimentally (cf. 17, 30, 58), and several conclusions
seem pretty clear. One is that reinforcement should be
positive rather than negative, constructive rather than
destructive. Reinforcement should be immediate. If it
is delayed, the trainee's motivation may lag, and also,
the reinforcement fails to provide information which he
may need in order to learn anything.

As the effects of delay imply, reinforcement
appears to serve two functions. One is to sustain motivation, and the other is to provide information, or feedback. According to some writers this feedback or
information value of reinforcement is the only function
which the consequences of behavior serve (42). Other
theorists ever since Thorndike have contended that the
function of reinforcement is in some way to "stamp in"
in some literal sense the stimulus-response association.
According to this latter view, reinforcement has little
or no effect as far as information is concerned. Whatever the truth of this matter may be, it appears

practically reasonable and profitable to administer reinforcement as though its informational value were important. There is ample evidence to show that a trainee's
performance may be improved if his scores are reported
to him, or if his performance is described and he is en-
couraged to make improvement (25). It has been found,
in fact, that this is one of the most effective ways in
which behavior of the trainee can be modified.

A great deal of attention has been paid in recent
years notably by Skinner and his students, to the fact that
performance is apt to be facilitated if reinforcement is
made probabilistic (37). It has been found that under
some conditions subjects will work harder if they are
reinforced only once in a while rather than upon every
occurrence of the desired behavior. It appears, however, that this phenomenon occurs only with respect to
performance, and that it is not reflected in superior
learning under partial or intermittent reinforcement.
It seems doubtful that transfer to a new situation would
be improved by this kind of reinforcement schedule. At
present, there seems to be no contrary evidence to the
general conclusion that learning is facilitated by frequent,
immediate, and positive reinforcement.

Set

The factors of set and attention are frequently
mentioned by writers on the subject of human learning.
In fact, even the layman would be disinclined to quarrel
with such statements as "the learner must be set for
learning," or "the learner must pay attention." Yet the
scientific literature concerning the effects of these factors on learning is not at all voluminous.

An excellent review of the topic of set was made
by Gibson (15) in 1941, in which it was shown that the
term has had a variety of meanings in psychological

experiments. This is still true today. Nevertheless, a
most instructive general meaning has been attributed to
the word set by Hebb (16), which can be considered as
incorporating several of the apparently disparate meanings identified by Gibson. Hebb considers set to be a
central neural mechanism comparable to a holding circuit. It is a persisting activity which is set up within
the central system, and which has its motor effect only
when a second sensory input occurs, with which it acts
to produce a response. As a simple example, if we say
to an individual "Add these numbers," and then provide
him with various sets of numbers, each of the responses
will represent his attempt at adding (not subtracting,
multiplying, or something else).

In a learning situation, one can think of establishing a task set by such instructions as "Listen to
these pairs of names, and be ready to say the second one
of each pair when I give you the first." Of course, as
Gibson points out, a set of this sort might be established
in ways other than by instructions, for example, by previous training or sequencing of events. But its importance for learning should not be overlooked or dismissed
lightly.

The factor of task set is apparently the same as
Thorndike's factor of belonging (41), by which he meant
the learner's knowledge of "what goes with what."
Thorndike performed a series of experiments having the
following general pattern. First, he instructed subjects
to listen to series of orally-presented materials, such
as pairs like "afford 21; equip 34" (in a long list), paying attention as they would if listening to a lecture. After
running through the list, in which specific pairs occurred
with different frequencies, he then asked the subjects to
write the answers to questions like "What number came
after 'afford'? " and in contrast, to questions such as
"What word came after 21? " Evidences of considerable

learning were obtained in answers to the first type of question, in which the pairs seem to "belong" together. But almost no learning was found to have occurred between the pairs, because, he argued, there was no "belonging. " Thorndike points out that this evidence demonstrates the inadequacy of sheer contiguity or sheer repetition for learning. Belonging, or what we call a task set, must be present.

In practical training situations, inexperienced teachers may unknowingly violate this principle of task set. In the training of complex tasks, the teacher may state the ultimate goal of learning (for example, to learn to operate a control panel), and then proceed to "set the student free" to practice. But the principle of task set applies to the individual items to be learned, and in such circumstances the student may have to engage in a great deal of needless trial and error behavior before discovering for himself "what goes with what" (for example, that a particular knob controls the activity of a particular dial). The importance of this principle is, therefore, that to maximize learning efficiency means must be found, usually by instructions, to establish suitable task sets to each of the items of the total task to be learned. Attending to the stimuli which are relevant, as defined by the final task to be performed, is an important condition for the assurance of a high degree of transfer.

Attention; Intent to Learn

The factor of attention in learning may be conceived in two different ways. The first, which we wish to exclude from consideration in this section, refers to the arousal of a general state of alertness (as opposed, perhaps, to drowsiness) in the learner. Although attention in the sense of alertness has been investigated in many ways (e. g. , 19, 20), it is of interest to note that none of the references in an extensive bibliography on

attention (22) identifies a study which is unequivocally
concerned with the relationship of alertness to learning
or transfer. It is apparent, therefore, that we simply
do not know the significance of this kind of "attentional"
variable; nor do we have any particular theoretical basis
on which to make predictions about it.

Intention to learn, on the other hand, has been
studied quite extensively. In contrast to the task set
described previously, intention to learn is typically induced by instructions that the materials presented are to
be committed to memory, as opposed to being simply
read, pronounced, or attended to in some other manner.
The technique of contrasting the performance of one
group of individuals who are told to learn, with that of
other indiviudals who act as "experimenters, " and thus
repeat the same materials without being told to learn
them, is common in modern experiments.

A review of previous studies on intent to learn
is given by McGeoch and Irion (26, p. 210 ff.). A recent
series of studies has been conducted by Postman and his
associates (31, 32, 33, 34, 35, 36). These studies have
utilized criteria of learning that are relevant to learning
efficiency, including measures of retention and retroactive interference, thereby on some occasions obtaining
results that contrast sharply with those obtained from
simpler situation-bound measures of learning.

Perhaps somewhat surprisingly from the view-
point of popular belief, the general findings of studies of
incidental learning are to the effect that intent to learn is
not always, or even usually, an important factor in learning (32, 33, 35). While some particular materials are
learned slightly better by those with intent to learn, the
incidental learners sometimes perform equally well.
Furthermore, associative interference is often reduced
under incidental learning conditions, thus actually making

the retention of incidentally-learned materials superior
to intentionally-learned ones on some occasions. We are
led to the conclusion that intent to learn has not been
shown to be a factor worthy of much concern in considering manipulable variables in a training situation. It
should, of course, be carefully distinguished from motivation to succeed, the significance of which has been discussed previously.

Associative Factors

When we turn to a consideration of associative
factors in learning efficiency, we need to consider the
variables affecting the nature of what is to be learned.
More specifically, these are the number, order, and
nature of associative connections that can be manipulated
within the learning situation. As stated previously, we
are here considering learning in terms of performance
of a final task which is not necessarily the same as the
"materials to be learned." This means that we must
deal with variables that have been investigated in connection with transfer of training, and not simply learning
itself.

In all, we shall consider here three classes of
factors in relation to learning efficiency. The first is
what is to be associated, or the nature of the associations
to be established, considered in relation to the task on
which performance is desired. The second is intra-trial
factors, or those conditions which may be varied systematically within each trial of learning, applying equally to
all trials. The third is inter-trial factors, which may be
manipulated in some orderly way between learning trials,
or in stages as learning proceeds.

The Nature of Associations

The most important characteristics of

associations to be learned, if we keep in mind the transfer of learning to a criterion task, pertain to similarity.
This factor has been subjected to a fair amount of investigation which has been summarized in standard works
(cf. 17, 26). Osgood (29) has made an attempt to system-
atize the empirical data in terms of a "transfer-retroaction
surface," which shows the relationship between similarity
of stimuli and similarity of responses to amount of transfer of training.

Stimulus similarity. Concerning the factor of
stimulus similarity there has never been any serious
disagreement of experimental evidence with the following
rule: Positive transfer increases with the degree of
similarity of the stimuli of the initially learned task to
the final task (17, 30). Thus the significance of this
principle for learning efficiency is clear; stimuli of the
associations to be learned should be made as nearly like
the stimuli of the final task as possible. In terms of
practical training situations, this principle may well be
tempered by feasibility. For example, if an operator
must learn to identify the switches, knobs and dials on
a panel, can these be represented in photographs (or
even drawings) rather than as three-dimensional objects?
The answer appears to be that high amounts of positive
transfer may be obtained by representations of stimulus
objects (10). This means that the stimuli to be associated
in the learning situation can be pictured, rather than
"real," without great losses in transfer; and this finding
has considerable practical significance for military
training. On the other hand, providing simply conceptual
representation for stimuli, as is done when words are
used rather than pictures, is another matter entirely;
and in such instances the principle of stimulus "similarity"
may in fact be violated. A picture of an amplifier may
be highly similar to the amplifier itself, but the word
"amplifier" as a stimulus is by no means similar. In
any case, the principle of stimulus similarity is not one

on which the books can or should be closed; it will require
a great deal more research to provide precise meaning
to this phrase.

Response similarity. It would be convenient
indeed if we could state that there is a comparable rule
about the response members of the associations established by learning, namely, that transfer of training
increases with the degree of similarity of responses of
the initially learned task and the final task. But although
Osgood's treatment (29) of the matter would support this
conclusion, we cannot agree that this principle should be
considered well-established. There are several reasons
for this:

1. Generally speaking, it is known that the
mediating responses for motor acts, acquired in initial
learning, need not be highly similar to these motor acts
in order for high degrees of transfer to occur. If an
individual is able to identify the location of objects in a
picture by pointing to them, we expect that he can also
walk to them correctly when he is at the actual scene of
the picture. Yet the responses in this initial and final
task are really quite different (cf. 10). There are not
many experiments in this field, probably because the
facts have appeared so obvious.

2. Most of the evidence on response similarity
has been obtained with the learning of paired associates,
and some of the crucial evidence comes from studies
employing responses which are similar in meaning
(cf. 28). The difficulty may be, that the second member
(often called the "response member") of a pair of associates has a stimulus function, as well as being employed
as a response. As a consequence, it interacts with other
members which are similar in meaning, and thus has an
effect on transfer. But this meaningful similarity is
behaving as a mediating stimulus, rather than as a

response pure and simple. How else, in fact, could
meaningful similarity of responses be interpreted? That
the "response member" both functions as a response and
enters into learning as a stimulus is shown by a study of
Feldman and Underwood (9).

        3. The results of paired associate learning are
strongly influenced by intra-list interference, as has
been demonstrated by many studies (13, 14, 43, 44, 47,
48). It seems particularly doubtful that one can draw
valid conclusions about 1st task--2nd task similarity
unless intra-task similarity has been measured separately or ruled out completely. An analysis by Gagné and
Baker (11) points out the importance of intra-task similarity to transfer. It is probable, therefore, that the
empirical results obtained on response similarity in
paired associate learning are quite inadequate for significant conclusions to be drawn concerning the effects of
this factor on single associations in learning.

        Response similarity has been demonstrated as
a factor affecting response strength in studies of generalization (55, 56), as well as in studies of motor skills (1).
But this evidence is an inadequate basis for the derivation
of principles of learning of verbal and conceptual tasks.
In view of this, and the objections raised to existing
evidence as listed above, we must conclude that response
similarity is a factor concerning which we know very
little.   The question of learning efficiency requires a
good deal more systematic knowledge regarding the
effects of this variable.

        Similarity in serial tasks. Some special mention
needs to be made of the effects of similarity of associated
items in sequentially-learned materials, which are relevant particularly to job tasks of following procedures.
In such tasks, each element clearly functions as a response and also as a stimulus to be associated with the

next succeeding response in the series. As a number of
investigations have shown (cf. 46, 50), the learning of
sequential verbal material is influenced both by intra-
task similarities and by the similarities of the learning
task to the final task. In fact, the separation of these
two effects has not yet been satisfactorily determined (51).

The learning of sequential verbal tasks increases
in rate as the individual members are made less similar
to each other. This suggests that when we have a procedural task characterized by associative interference,
the mediating task provided for learning may be facilitated
by making the associated members less similar to each
other than those of the procedural task itself. In other
words, it seems possible that the members of the learning task may be made more distinctive than the members
of the final task, and thus increase learning efficiency.
However, it should be remembered that although the
effects of such intra-task variation are predictable, we
do not know what effects this treatment would have on
inter-task interference; in other words, we do not know
its effects on transfer to a job task. It is apparent that,
so far as following procedures are concerned, the interplay of similarities among elements and between initial
and final tasks is an area in which considerable additional research is needed.

Intra-Trial Factors

In continuing our consideration of associative
factors, we next turn to a set of variables that may be
manipulated within each and every trial of learning. As
we have pointed out previously, these are to be distinguished from variables which are systematically varied
from trial to trial, or in stages as learning progresses.
There are three primary ways in which such intra-trial
factors may be manipulated, and we shall discuss them
here. For any given response, the stimuli to be

associated with it may be varied in number and variety.
Second, for any particular stimulus, the individual may
be required to learn different numbers of responses.
And third, the meaningfulness of the associations may be
varied.

Number of stimuli. We can adduce little evidence
from the experimental literature concerning this factor
and its influence on transfer of training. The experimental question may be described as follows. Suppose
we are interested in the performance of an identification
task of fifteen components (such as, the components of a
newly-developed weapon). In a standard learning situation we would expose a picture of each item and require
the learner to respond with its name. However, being
aware of the effects of similarity in producing associative
interference, and thus decreasing the rate of learning,
we might decide to add additional stimuli to each pictured
item, in order to make them more distinctive from each
other. Increased distinctiveness, for example, might
be added by accompanying each item with a distinctive
color, a distinctive symbol, a distinctive border, etc.
It is sometimes argued that the effect of this added number and variety of stimuli would be to reduce associative
interference and thus speed up the learning. The question
as to whether transfer to the final task would be as good
or better under these conditions needs to be answered
by experimental investigation. The idea of providing
extra "stimulus support" for learning is one of the hypotheses that appears to be involved in the work of
Skinner (6, 39) on teaching machines.

Number of responses. This is another factor
concerning which no direct experimental evidence exists.
Using the fifteen-item identification task as an example
again, the standard learning situation in which each
stimulus is associated with a single response (e. g. , a
name) may be contrasted with one in which additional

responses are also required to be learned to the same stimulus. For example, we might require the learner to acquire the responses "square," "black," "voltage," as well as "amplifier" to a picture of an amplifier. Presumably, it would take him longer to learn four responses to each stimulus item than it would for him to learn one. Nevertheless, the experimental question of importance to learning efficiency concerns the matter of the effects of this variable on transfer of training. If the criterion of transfer is employed, it is entirely conceivable that the added effort (and time) required for initial learning might be overbalanced by advantages in transfer of training.

Of some relevance to this question may be the studies which have shown increasing degrees of positive transfer when increasing numbers of verbal lists are learned (cf. 26, p. 306 ff.). Underwood and Richardson's study (52), for example, measured transfer in the learning of a series of paired-adjective lists, in which each successive list required the learning of different responses to the same stimuli. The number of trials required to learn a test list (a measure of transfer) decreased regularly with the number of preceding lists learned. Thus transfer was found to be an increasing function of the number of previously acquired responses to stimuli.

Also relevant to this question may be the results on meaningfulness, to be discussed below. There can be little doubt about the faster learning of meaningful materials, although an advantage in recall does not appear (53). Noble (27) hypothesizes a direct relationship between meaningfulness and number of associated responses. If one accepts this notion, then the superior efficiency of meaningful learning materials may be attributed to the greater number of previously acquired associations such stimuli have. Another implication is that the meaningfulness of stimuli (and thus their transfer effectiveness) may be manipulated in the learning situation by requiring the learner to acquire a number of responses to the stimulus. Skinner's (6, 39) technique of "ringing the changes" on a particular principle to be learned may also be basically a matter of increasing the number of responses to single stimuli.

Notwithstanding the existence of this rather indirect experimental evidence, there remains a need for research directly aimed at finding an answer to this question about number of responses and transfer. The possibility exists that requiring the learning of increased numbers of responses to the same stimuli may be a significant factor in learning efficiency, insofar as it can increase positive transfer.

Meaningfulness. As is well known, many investigations of human learning have been concerned with nonsense materials. Frequently, research is conducted with materials for which meaningfulness is held as a constant, preferably low, value. But there is considerable evidence that meaningful materials are learned more rapidly than are nonsense materials. In fact the differences in learning usually found in favor of meaningful materials imply that this is a factor of outstanding importance to learning efficiency (cf. 5, 26). The question of learning efficiency, which has not been diectly investigated, may be stated as follows: (1) Given a set of inherently meaningless identifications to be made in a job task, can transfer be most effectively mediated by the acquisition of meaningful associations? (2) Given a more or less meaningless sequence of acts to be performed in following a procedure, can transfer be insured by acquiring a meaningful verbal sequence representing these acts? (3) What effect does degree of meaningfulness of concepts acquired in a learning situation have upon the performance of "concept-using" tasks including problem solving?

The experimental evidence (cf. 17, 26) shows, first of all, that there is a regular increase in rapidity of learning as the material to be learned increases in meaningfulness. This effect is enhanced when the members being associated are connected by some logical sequence. There is a definite relationship between this finding and the long-known effectiveness of mnemonic systems (see references in McGeoch and Irion, 26, p. 478). Cofer's findings (3) on the retention of meaningful materials show that learned concepts may be acquired (as "ideas") much more rapidly than can exact verbal passages, and that they continue to function as concepts for a long time after exact verbal sequences have been forgotten. This finding is consistent with the suggestion of certain writers (18, 30) that mediation by means of meaningful materials may be most economical of learning time because a small absolute amount of material must be acquired. Putting all these things together, there is some doubt that meaningfulness has ever been accorded quite the importance it deserves as a factor in learning within the framework of traditional investigations. Further, the transfer value of meaningful materials has only rarely been emphasized (18).

Inter-Trial Factors

There are two general kinds of factors which may be varied between trials of learning. One of these is the temporal distribution of trials or practice sessions, and the other is change in the learning task.

Massed or distributed practice. The question of whether practice is more efficient if trials are massed or if they are distributed is a classical problem which has been studied extensively (58). Basically, it is clear that if the inter-trial interval is too long, everything that has been learned on the preceding trial tends to be forgotten and to have to be relearned on the next trial.

Even partial forgetting implies that some relearning could be avoided by reducing the interval between trials. On the other hand, closely massed trials are likely to produce fatigue, boredom, and work decrement. In this latter case, however, it is not altogether certain that the decrements so typically displayed actually indicate a retardation of learning. Some studies (7, 21) suggest rather strongly that the decrements apply only to the performance, not to the learning. When rest intervals and a suitable test are introduced following the period of learning, it is found that massed practice groups have actually acquired more than they have demonstrated during learning. Thus massed learning is more efficient than it would appear. Probably the main effect of massed practice is upon motivation rather than on association. Several studies of serial learning (17, 45) have found that performance is facilitated to a greater extent by increasing the time per item during the presentation, than by introducing rest intervals between repetitions of the list. This finding suggests that the most efficient learning program, in terms of total elapsed time, may be one in which material is presented slowly within each trial, but massed in the sense that one trial promptly follows another. Finally, there are studies (4, 8) which have suggested that when the task to be learned is a very difficult one, inhibitory effects of massing trails may be more than offset by the difficulty of remembering pro-cedural details from one trial to the next.

If we conceive of the intra-trial interval as being important because it relates to the ease with which the learner can proceed in learning, one obvious solution would be to let the trainee set his own intra-trial interval, that is, let him pace himself. Skinner has argued that this is one virtue of his teaching machines (38, 39). It may well be that the learner is the best possible judge of his own level of inhibition and his own best judge of when he is ready to proceed in learning. With such a self-pacing procedure it is usually found that the subject chooses a relatively long intra-trial interval early in learning, and decreases this interval as learning proceeds. Again we must note that the temporal sequencing of training which leads to the most efficient transfer to the job situation needs to be determined by experimental study.

Task scheduling. A more complex question concerns how the relevant stimuli should be scheduled. There appear to be two distinct schools of thought on the subject. One of these (18, 54) contends that the underlying principle (or the crucial stimulus element) with which the behavior is to be associated should be emphasized from the first, and should serve as a stable reference point throughout the course of learning. According to such a position, departure from this procedure can only lead to interference and learning decrement. In practice, however, this procedure has the disadvantage of frustrating the learner if he cannot make the correct responses at the outset. On the other hand, Skinner, among others, has maintained that the desired response should be given every possible stimulus support from the outset of learning (6, 39). The purpose of this stimulus support is to insure that the correct response will be made. Once made, it can then be reinforced, and the superfluous stimuli gradually removed. The obvious difficulty with this strategy is that it is quite likely that the reinforcement will strengthen the association of the response to the wrong stimulus. Which procedure leads to the greatest efficiency of learning and the greatest transfer to a new situation, is not presently known.

It seems likely that superiority of one or the other procedure may depend upon many factors. If the correct response is a verbal one, if it can be elicited by instruction or by some other means, and if a suitable task set can draw the trainee's attention to the relevant stimulus, then this would seem to suffice. However, it is clear that there are many learning situations in which all these things cannot be done. This is true, for example, when the correct response and the relevant stimulus cannot be verbally communicated to the trainee. We may note in this connection Skinner's method of using extra "stimulus supports" is derived by analogy from his animal studies. While he argues for the efficacy of this method in teaching machines, we do not know that the two procedures have been put to a critical test. One obvious disadvantage of Skinner's procedure is that once the response has been established in the presence of a number of stimuli, it is then necessary to eliminate the irrelevant stimuli from the total stimulus complex, in order that only the relevant one will remain in association with the desired response. This means that learning must proceed as a discrimination problem in which the relevant stimulus must be discriminated from the irrelevant ones, or else the danger is run that the trainee will conclude his training having learned something irrelevant. Thus, there is the possibility that additional training is required, over that which is really necessary for the desired performance, before the trainee is in a position to go into the transfer situation. Those who uphold Skinner's position might well argue at this point that the superfluous stimulus support given the correct response early in learning can be gradually withdrawn so that the overall learning efficiency is not impaired. This argument fails to recognize, however, that these irrelevant stimuli not only support the correct response but also incorrect and competing responses which may introduce interference. As an example of this problem consider learning of the touch system of typing. The question we are considering may be phrased as follows: Can the touch system of typing be learned better if (1) the names of the keys are present, or (2) if the keys are blank? Most educators seem to agree that while the presence of the letter names on the keys is an aid in early learning, they may actually impede the ultimate level of proficiency desired in touch typing.   More research needs to be done before any clearcut answer to this question can be obtained.

Wolfle has pointed out (57) that in any instance of stimulus-response learning, if the contextual stimuli remain constant through the course of learning, they will all tend to become (irrelevantly) associated with the correct response.   On the basis of evidence from several studies, he is led to conclude that a desirable condition for efficient learning would involve the use of a variety of contextual stimulus conditions, in which only the relevant stimulus remains invariant.   The evidence indicates that learning under these variable conditions is indeed less resistant to extinction than is learning under constant stimulus conditions.   Such evidence appears quite inconsistent with what a "stimulus support" principle would lead us to expect.

Summary and Conclusions

We have attempted in this report to identify the manipulable conditions of learning which may be used to insure maximum transfer from learning to tasks of the job.   This is the meaning we have used here for the phrase learning efficiency.   In considering this question, we first distinguish three kinds of tasks found in the Air Force for which learning is required.   These three are identification, procedure following, and concept using. For these kinds of performance, we have described and discussed the evidence regarding training variables which are likely to lead to maximal learning efficiency.

On the whole, our conclusion from this evidence must be that there are few principles which can be directly applied to the problem of making learning efficient. The findings concerning the nature of the learning process in human beings are primarily suggestive for this problem, rather than productive of verified practical rules for the control of conditions of efficient learning. This means that the attempt to manipulate learning conditions, whether carried out by a teacher or by the designer of a teaching machine, must employ a good deal of art and not much science, at the present stage of knowledge.

On the other hand, our review of the factors in efficient learning shows us that there are quite a number of these factors which may, in any given situation, be manipulated to affect learning efficiency. If these could all be systematically controlled by means of a machine, or by an otherwise well-designed learning situation, the possibilities of increasing the efficiency of learning over that which typically results from practical training appear great indeed. A suitably designed machine could, of course, be used to carry out such a program of research. Estimates can be made of the relative importance of these factors we have described to learning efficiency. But to attain the goal of ultimate control over learning, it is even more important to undertake research which will determine how far each of these variables, or combinations of them, can be pushed in making learning efficient. As we have pointed out, such a question is neither asked nor answered by the conventional experimental study of human learning.

References

1. Baker, K. E. , Wylie, R. C. , and Gagné, R. M. , Transfer of training to a motor skill as a function of variation in rate of response. J. exp. Psychol. , 1950, 40, 721-732.

2. Bolles, R. C. , The usefulness of the drive concept. In Jones, M. R. (ed.), Nebraska symposium on Motivation. Lincoln, Nebr. : University of Nebraska Press, 1958.

3. Cofer, C. N. , A comparison of logical and verbatum learning of prose passages of different lengths. Amer. J. Psychol. , 1941, 54, 1-20.

4. Cook, T. W. , Factors in massed and distributed practice. J. exp. Psychol. , 1944, 34, 325-334.

5. Davis, R. A. , Psychology of Learning. New York: McGraw-Hill, 1935.

6. Edwards, W. , Skinner's teaching machines. Laboratory Note ML-LN-56-3, Maintenance Laboratory, Air Force Personnel and Training Research Center, May 1956 (unpublished communication).

7. Epstein, B. , Immediate and retention effects of interpolated rest periods on learning performance. Teach. Coll. Contr. Educ. , No. 949, 1949.

8. Ericksen, S. C. , Variability of attack in massed and distributed practice. J. exp. Psychol. , 1942, 31, 339-345.

9. Feldman, S. M. , and Underwood, B. J. , Stimulus recall following paired-associate learning. J. exp. Psychol. , 1957, 53, 11-15.

10. Gagne, R. M. , and Foster, H. , Transfer to a motor skill from practice on a pictured representation. J. exp. Psychol. , 1949, 39, 342-355.

11. Gagne, R. M. , and Baker, K. E. , On the relation between similarity and transfer of training in the learning of discriminative motor tasks. Psychol. Rev. , 1950, 57, 67-79.

12. Gibson, E. J., A systematic application of the concepts of generalization and differentiation to verbal learning. Psychol. Rev., 1940, 47, 196-229.

13. Gibson, E. J., Retroactive inhibition as a function of degree of generalization between tasks. J. exp. Psychol., 1941, 28, 93-115.

14. Gibson, E. J., Intra-list generalization as a factor in verbal learning. J. exp. Psychol., 1942, 30, 185-200.

15. Gibson, J. J., A critical review of the concept of set in contemporary experimental psychology. Psychol. Bull., 1941, 38, 781-817.

16. Hebb, D. O., A textbook of psychology. Philadelphia: Saunders, 1958.

17. Hovland, C. I., Human learning and retention. In S. S. Stevens (ed.) Handbook of experimental psychology. New York: Wiley, 1951.

18. Katona, G., Organizing and memorizing. New York: Columbia Univ. Press, 1940.

19. Kennedy, J. L., and Travis, R. C., Prediction of speed of performance by muscle action potentials. Science. 1947, 105, 410-411.

20. Kennedy, J. L., and Travis, R. C., Prediction and control of alertness: II. Continuous tracking. J. comp. physiol. Psychol., 1948, 41, 203-210.

21. Kientzle, M. J., Ability patterns under distributed practice, J. exp. Psychol., 1949, 39, 532-537.

22. Kreezer, G. L., Hill, J. H. and Manning W., Attention. A bibliography and classification of the psychological literature. Wright Air Development Center, WADC Technical Report 54-455, August, 1954.

23. Lewin, K., Dembo, T., Festinger, L., and Sears, P. S., Level of aspiration. Ch. 10 in Hunt, J. McV., Personality and the behavior disorders. Vol. I. New York: Ronald Press, 1944.

24. Littman, R. A., Motives, history, and causes. In Jones, M. R. (ed.), Nebraska symposium on motivation. Lincoln, Nebr.: University of Nebraska Press, 1958.

25. MacPherson, S. J., Dees, V., and Grindley, G. C., The effect of knowledge of results on learning and performance. II, III. Quart. J. exp. Psychol., 1948, 1949, 1, 68-78, 167-174.

26. McGeoch, J. A., and Irion, A. L., The psychology of human learning (2nd ed.). New York: Longmans, Green and Company, 1952.

27. Noble, C. E., An analysis of meaning. Psychol. Rev., 1952, 59, 421-430.

28. Osgood, C. E., Meaningful similarity and interference in learning. J. exp. Psychol., 1946, 36, 277-301.

29. Osgood, C. E., The similarity paradox in human learning: A resolution. J. exp. Psychol., 1949, 56, 132-143.

30. Osgood, C. E., Method and theory in experimental psychology. New York: Oxford Univ. Press, 1953.

31. Postman, L. , and Phillips, L. W. , Studies in incidental learning: I. The effects of crowding and isolation. J. exp. Psychol. , 1954, 48, 48-56.

32. Postman, L. , Adams,· P. A. , and Phillips, L. W. , Studies in incidental learning: II. The effects of association value and of the method of testing. J. exp. Psychol. , 1955, 49, 1-10.

33. Postman, L. , and Adams, P. A. , Studies in incidental learning: III. Interserial interference. J. exp. Psychol. , 1956, 51, 323-328.

34. Postman, L. , and Adams, P. A. , Studies in incidental learning: IV. The interaction of orienting tasks and stimulus materials. J. exp. Psychol. , 1956, 51, 329-342.

35. Postman, L. , Adams, P. A. , and Bohm, A. M. , Studies in incidental learning: V. Recall for order and associative clustering. J. exp. Psychol. 1956, 51, 334-342.

36. Postman, L. , and Adams, P. A. , Studies in incidental learning: VI. Intraserial interference. J. exp. Psychol. , 1956, 54, 153-167.

37. Skinner, B. F. , Science and human behavior. New York: Macmillan, 1953.

38. Skinner, B. F. , The science of learning and the art of teaching. Harvard Educ. Rev. , 1954, 24, 86-97.

39. Skinner, B. F. , Teaching machines. Science, 1958, 128, 969-977.

40. Spence, K. W. , Behavior Theory and Conditioning.
    New Haven: Yale University Press, 1956.

41. Thorndike, E. L. , The fundamentals of learning.
    New York: Teachers College, Columbia
    University, 1932.

42. Tolman, E. C. , Hall, C. S. , and Bretnall, E. P. ,
    A disproof of the law of effect and a substitution
    of the laws of emphasis, motivation, and
    disruption. J. exp. Psychol. , 1932, 15, 601-614.

43. Underwood, B. J. , and Goad, D. , Studies of
    distributed practice: I. The influence of intra-
    list similarity in verbal learning. J. exp. Psychol. ,
    1951, 42, 125-134.

44. Underwood, B. J. , Studies of distributed practice: II.
    Learning and retention of paired-adjective lists
    with two levels of intra-list similarity.
    J. exp. Psychol. , 1951, 42, 153-161.

45. Underwood, B. J. , and Viterna, R. O. , Studies of
    distributed practice: IV. The effect of similarity
    and rate of presentation in verbal-discrimination
    learning. J. exp. Psychol. , 1951, 42, 296-299.

46. Underwood, B. J. , Studies of distributed practice:
    VII. Learning and retention of serial nonsense lists
    as a function of intra-list similarity.
    J. exp. Psychol. , 1952, 44, 80-87.

47. Underwood, B. J. , Studies of distributed practice:
    VIII. Learning and retention of paired non-
    sense syllables as a function of intra-list
    similarity. J. exp. Psychol. , 1953, 45, 133-142.

48. Underwood, B. J. , Studies of distributed practice:
    IX. Learning and retention of paired adjectives
    as a function of intra-list similarity.
    J. exp. Psychol. , 1953, 45, 143-149.

49. Underwood, B. J. , Studies of distributed practice:
    X. The influence of intra-list similarity on
    learning and retention of serial adjective lists.
    J. exp. Psychol., 1953, 45, 253-259.

50. Underwood, B. J. , Studies of distributed practice:
    XI. An attempt to resolve conflicting facts on
    retention of serial nonsense lists.
    J. exp. Psychol. , 1953, 45, 355-359.

51. Underwood, B. J. ; Intralist similarity in verbal
    learning and retention. Psychol. Rev. , 1954,
    61, 160-166.

52. Underwood, B. J. , and Richardson, J. , Studies of
    distributed practice: XIII. Inter-list interference
    and the retention of serial nonsense lists.
    J. exp. Psychol. , 1955, 50, 39-46.

53. Underwood, B. J. , and Richardson, J. , The influ-
    ence of meaningfulness, intra-list similarity,
    and serial position on retention. J. exp. Psychol.,
    1956, 52, 119-126.

54. Wertheimer, M. , Productive thinking. New York:
    Harper, 1945.

55. Wickens, D. D. , Studies of response generalization
    in conditioning: I. Stimulus generalization
    during response generalization. J. exp. Psychol. ,
    1943, 33, 221-227.

56. Wickens, D. D., Studies of response generalization in conditioning: II. The comparative strength of the transferred and non-transferred responses. J. exp. Psychol., 1943, 33, 330-332.

57. Wolfle, D., Training. In S. S. Stevens (ed.), Handbook of experimental psychology. New York: Wiley, 1951, 1267-1286.

58. Woodworth, R. S., and Schlosberg, H., Experimental psychology (Rev. Ed.). New York: Holt, 1954.

3

Jacob Beck

University of Pennsylvania

ON SOME METHODS

OF PROGRAMMING

This paper presents some systematic concepts concerning the preparation of material for an exposure device similar to the type originally designed by Skinner.

Many scientists acquainted with the problems of constructing teaching programs have accepted the objective that one should present material in such a way as to minimize the probability of an incorrect response. Others maintain that an optimum error rate would be advantageous. However, all have recognized that an essential feature of the teaching process is that a student's responses are guided and restricted in ways that will facilitate the occurrence of the correct response.

The means of achieving this direction in the construction of a teaching program are, however, unclear. A student's responses may be restricted and guided in a great number of different ways. These range from all types of hints and prompts--either formal or based upon relevant behavioral processes--to simply presenting the response which it is desired a student acquire. In order to compare the different possible teaching programs it is necessary to develop a classification which distinguishes their essential features. The development of such a classification is facilitated by representing the different ways of restricting responses as teaching rules.

Teaching rules describe the way a student's responses are controlled. They can differ in the degree to which they restrict behavior, the way in which they restrict behavior, whether they involve stimuli in addition to the discriminative stimuli which set the occasion for the response and whether they are explicit or implicit. Examples of some broad classes of teaching rules that involve the presentation of additional stimuli are copying, analogy, and deductive rules. A copying rule restricts the student to copying one of a specifiable number of alternative responses that are presented. A student's responses are completely restricted if only one, the correct response, is presented. To take a simple illustration: in teaching spelling, the word to be learned can appear spelled correctly for the student to copy.

Analogy and deductive rules present additional stimulus material (such as spelling analogues and spelling rules) from which the student can obtain the correct response by drawing an analogy or a logical deduction. A different possibility is to present the discriminative stimulus without any additional stimuli. In this case, a student's responses are restricted only by implicit rules of thumb he may have developed concerning different properties of the discriminative stimulus--such as the spelling of certain sounds. All types of prompts connected with the discriminative stimulus--e. g. , breaking up a word to be spelled into syllables and accentuating the pronounciation of each syllable--may, of course, be used.

Many other types of teaching rules can be identified, as for example, rules using different kinds of controlled association. Different teaching rules not only restrict responses in different ways, but also establish different mediating responses. These mediating responses may be taken as a basis to distinguish types of learning. Rote learning can be thought of as the learning of a stimulus-response connection by means of a copying rule.

Thus, a teaching rule depends on what one desires to teach. It may be a specific response: teaching a student to mark a statement true or false, or a set of facts: teaching a student a set of conditional responses, or problem solving: teaching a student to make related responses in related situations; all of these are different teaching rules. Before exploring further how different rules might be used, it would be helpful to characterize the teaching process so as to reveal other variables that are involved. The problem of motivation will not be considered in the following analysis.

The teaching process can be analyzed into several distinct components: (1) a discriminative stimulus which sets the occasion for the desired response, (2) the response which it is desired an individual acquire, (3) a rule or rules--explicit or implicit, with or without additional stimuli--that guide the student's responses, (4) reinforcement of the correct response. A teaching device will be called "controlled" if it specifies these components of the teaching process and at all times calls for a definite response on the part of the student relevant to the stimulus material presented. Otherwise it will be called "uncontrolled." The lack of control may vary in degree.

Traditional teaching devices such as books and lectures are almost completely uncontrolled. The discriminative stimuli are not explicitly specified by these devices. A student when confronted with a long passage of content in a text or lecture consisting of definitions, examples, and qualifications is, in fact, often in the position of choosing and constructing the particular stimuli to which his responses are attached. Many a difficulty in teaching can be traced to students "focusing" on the wrong stimuli and attaching responses to them. Furthermore, texts and lectures do not specify the particular response which it is desired that an individual

acquire. Since they do not generally require the student
to make any response, little if anything, can be known
of the student's responses to the content presented. For
example, we do not generally know whether the student
is paying attention, nor do we know whether he has merely memorized the solution to a problem or learned the
steps involved in solving the problem. The rules which
guide a student's responses are also indefinite. A student's response may be the result of copying a response
from the text, drawing analogies from examples mentioned
or making deductions from statements contained in the
text. Reinforcement under these conditions is also a
haphazard matter--depending upon accident and self-
administration.

In comparison, a teaching device, like Skinner's,
which presents to a student a sequence of inputs to which
he responds in a specifiable way allows for control of the
teaching process. The relevant discriminative stimuli
may be isolated and placed in the input. The responses
to be brought under the control of these stimuli may be
specified and the student required to make them. Rules
can be given which will both restrict and guide a student's
responses in the manner desired. Differential reinforcement can be employed to bring the desired responses
under the control of the relevant stimuli.

Thus, two principle ways in which programs
prepared for a Skinner-type exposure device can differ
are: (1) their control or lack of control of the teaching
process and (2) the type of teaching rules they employ.
One can compare some of the programs which have already been constructed or suggested with respect to
these differences. These comparisons will be limited to
only the type of teaching rules employed and the kind of
additional stimuli presented. In all programs it will be
assumed that the relevant discriminative stimuli have
been specified and placed in the input, that the student

makes the response which it is desired he acquire and
not a substitute response, and that differential reinforcement operates.

One method of programming breaks up the material to be taught into a great number of carefully designed steps. In working through the program, the
student will first make a response and then compare his
response with the correct answer. If the two correspond,
the student adjusts the program in such a way as to delete
the stimulus item; if they do not correspond, the student
continues to the next step of the program but encounters
the stimulus item in working through the program a
second time, both explicit and implicit teaching rules
occur in such a program. The implicit rules can be of
various kinds. They include all the different kinds of
hints and prompts that can be included in stimulus items
for the express purpose of guiding a student's responses.
The explicit teaching rule employed in the program is a
type of copying rule in which the response copied is not
immediately present but is rather the response with
which the student compared his own in the previous exposure of the stimulus item. This method of programming
is controlled since the teaching rules are specified and
the student makes a definite response to all stimulus
material. However, because of the fact that successive
steps in this kind of program are often prompted by preceding items, the program has to break up the material
to be taught into a great number of small steps and is
usually of considerable length.

One might attempt to shorten the length of such
programs and further restrict students' responses by
means of a teaching rule that would introduce additional
stimuli relevant to the desired responses in the form of
content material. The stimulus items composing the
program could then cover larger portions of the subject
matter. A way of doing this would be to present the

student a handout to study containing, for instance, the specific responses which he will later be expected to make to stimulus items of the program. After studying the handout, the student could proceed through the program in the same way as previously described. However, a limitation of this method of programming is that it is teaching by means of a handout. This is similar to teaching by means of a text and is generally uncontrolled in all the ways previously discussed.

A procedure which would shorten the program and at the same time introduce the content material in a controlled way is to present the content together with the discriminative stimulus in a single stimulus item. The student is given an explicit rule which enables him to obtain the correct response from the content material. Thus, the student makes a definite response relevant to the content material presented. Since the content material is immediately present, a student using a copying rule would be certain to make the correct response by some definite number of responses. A student could, therefore, be required to make the correct response before proceeding to the next item. A student's responses are, however, made not only to the discriminative stimuli but also to the additional stimuli of the content material present. What one actually wants is that the responses be made only to the discriminative stimuli. Different teaching rules might, therefore, be combined in constructing a program employing content material in which the response is first made in the presence of the content material, but then the content material is reduced until the response is made without it.

The specific examples of programs thus far mentioned have mainly employed rules in which the student copies the correct response. Such a rule is probably most useful in teaching specific responses as are found in many skills. Often, however, what one

wants to teach is not a specific response but what would
commonly be called a fact. A fact can be thought of as
involving a large number of conditional responses. That
is, one would want a student to make one response under
one set of conditions and not make that response or even
make the opposite response under different conditions.
In this case it might well be that the most effective way
of teaching would be to have the student deduce these
responses from statements which clearly set forth the
conditions under which a given response would be correct
or incorrect rather than by simply copying the correct
response. In general, it would seem that a deductive
teaching rule would be most efficient where one is interested in either teaching deductive thinking itself or a
class of responses depending on specific properties or
relations. In problem solving it seems especially true
that the response that it is desired to teach is not a
specific one. What one wants to teach a student is to
make analogous responses in related situations. Thus,
what needs to be emphasized are the similarities and
differences of the conditions from one problem to another, and how these affect appropriate responses. A
way of doing this would be by the use of a teaching rule
based on the drawing of analogies. Clearly the problem
involved here is that of transfer. Both the deductive and
analogy teaching rules would, a priori, seem to be more
effective in establishing a basis for transfer than would
be a copying rule. With both these rules, an important
question becomes the number and kind of exemplars
necessary to teach a class of responses or a rule.

In the foregoing analysis many important problems of programming have not been discussed. One,
that should be mentioned here is that for practical reasons the student is often asked to make a response that
is not identical with the response it is desired he acquire.
A substitute response is introduced. For example, the
actual response in many programs is a single word

completing a statement rather than the statement itself.
If responses involving statements are to be recoded into
single words or pairs of words, an important question
becomes how this is to be done. Related to this is the
question of what actually is being reinforced. The conditions under which simpler responses can be substituted
for complicated responses is an important problem to
solve. Many, for instance, are interested in whether
true-false or multiple choice responses can be substituted
for constructive responses.

The foregoing analysis presents a scheme for
comparing different teaching programs. Whether or
not the classification proposed will prove significant
must, of course, await the performance of suitable
experiments.

4

B. F. Skinner

Harvard University

THE PROGRAMMING

OF VERBAL KNOWLEDGE

Several kinds of problems arise in the development of teaching machines: (1) What are the optimal physical dimensions of frames, sets, programs? What kinds of visual and auditory material can be tied in, and under what physical conditions? (2) How are programs related to overall curricula? What behavior in the student can be assumed by the programmer? Do individual differences require programs of different densities? (3) How are we to define and analyze a subject matter and determine a plausible sequence of steps leading from complete ignorance to complete competence? Temporary solutions to these problems can be found, for example, by simply programming a standard textbook for an existing type of machine, but other problems cannot be dismissed in this way.

The manipulation of the student's behavior is another area to be explored. How is the behavior in a given repertoire to be evoked for the first time, and how is it to be brought under the required stimulus control? Presumably experiments will be needed to determine (a) an optimal level of difficulty or, conversely, frequency of success, (b) an optimal frequency of recurrence of similar material for purposes of review, (c) an optimal frequency of "exercising" a controlling relation, (d) optimal schedules for seeding review material, (e) the possible use of relatively unrelated material to break up a too-powerful control by a given universe of discourse, (f) the optimal use of thematic and formal supporting material and the rate with which it is "vanished, " and so on.

Over and above all this, there is the problem of what is actually going on in the instructional situation. What kind of changes are we to bring about in the behavior of the student? How are these to be analyzed? And how are appropriate techniques to be found? The following comments apply to such questions.

Form of Verbal Response (Written)

Shaping a written response through the differential reinforcement of progressively more adequate forms is uncertain and inefficient. Indeed, it is impossible in a machine which reveals a correct response for comparison with a written, since a second try will be under the control of the previously revealed response and hence fall in the following category.

An available stimulus can be used to evoke the required response as part of the repertoire which the student brings to the machine. Instruction takes place only when the control exercised by the available stimulus is transferred to a new stimulus. This is what happens in teaching the spelling of a word by first showing it in its entirety and then having the student supply missing parts until he writes the whole word. It is also what happens in learning poetry, formulae, etc. , by reading a given sample and then almost immediately completing the sample when it is presented with parts missing. Larger samples of material involve setting up intraverbal behavior, rather than shaping up a form of response. The issue here is what "form of response" means. A whole poem or even a line is not a unit if it is learned as an intraverbal chain--nor is spelling a word, but intraverbal support may disappear, leaving what is essentially a patterned unit response.

The student may emit a response for the first time as the result of a process of construction. Thus, in learning the systematic vocabulary of chemistry, he may emit the response phosphorus pentachloride for the first time by mechanically combining roots and affixes under control of the symbols PCl_5. Other constructions involve syntactical arrangements of material acquired in other ways. Having learned the unit response ("fact") that "an atom is about one hundred millionth of a centimeter in diameter" the student can be expected to complete "the ---- of an atom is about one millionth of a centimeter," not because having been told the one he then knows the other, but because he has learned to translate from one syntactical frame to another. An important goal is to "enrich the student's understanding" by inducing him to permute and recombine the elements of his repertoire by similar syntactical revisions.

In the extreme case of syntactical and semantic variation, we may not be concerned with imparting any single verbal response under stimulus control or even an equivalent set of responses. The student will make one or more responses of such a set and be reinforced as right, but we are concerned with this only as evidence of other potential reactions. Suppose, for example, we illustrate and describe a simple model of the mass spectograph in an elementary course in college chemistry. There are many ways in which the student can describe the operation of the model correctly, but we are not concerned with setting up any one specific description. The student is to acquire, not an explicit verbal repertoire, but a variety of verbal responses which strongly suggest that he could operate the model, modify it for specific purposes, explain its operation to others, build such a model, and so on. We "make sure he understands the model" by asking him to complete sentences like "at point A a steel ball rolling down the inclined groove will be going at a speed which (is, is not) a function of its size." The form of his response will be determined by the illustration and the descriptive material, not because the same response recurs therein, but because translations into this form are possible. The goal is not to build the verbal repertoire itself, but to make sure that the student can correctly describe a state of affairs with responses already available in his repertoire with respect to similar states of affairs.

We may appeal to the same kind of free-floating repertoire in asking the student to comment upon a passage which he is to read, either before or while working on the machine material. A given response is right or wrong and is so indicated by the machine, but the immediate goal is not the shaping up of that particular form of response or bringing that response under specific control.

Bringing a Verbal Response Under the Control of Non-Verbal Stimuli

In instructing the student to identify the parts of maps, anatomical drawings, and so on, we present a non-verbal stimulus (picture, model, sample) along with the text for a verbal response. This is more than presenting a picture and a word together. A process of "instruction" (see 1) is involved. When a name appears printed on the outline of a country or on part of an anatomical drawing or beneath the picture of an object, the spatial arrangement has the effect of an autoclitic similar to This is an X. As a result the student is more powerfully affected by the juxtaposition. For efficient instruction, however, he must be induced to respond to the picture while reading the word. He can be induced to do this while engaging in useful behavior such as stating relationships, comparing pictures, describing details,

and so on. The text is then "vanished" at a suitable rate.
It may even be desirable to vanish the non-verbal stimulus. In the latter case the student can then describe the
object correctly even when it is not pictured or present.

Bringing a Verbal Response Under
Control of a Verbal Stimulus

In the simplest case two verbal stimuli are
presented together and responses evoked for some reason or other. It is more effective to connect the stimuli
with an explicit defining autoclitic, such as "X means X."
One verbal stimulus set off in apposition to another, or
after the word "or," is an implied definition. The result is not the mere learning of a vocabulary. Compare,
for example, a set of frames designed to acquaint the
student with the Greek prefixes for number. The set
might be used, for example, in teaching the systematic
vocabulary of chemistry. The student is to acquire the
correct use of mono, di, tri, tetra, penta, etc. , under
the control of numerical aspects of verbal and non-verbal
stimuli--e. g. , pictured polygons, or the subscripts in
chemical notations. Existing connections in the student's
repertoire can be exploited, going first from Greek to
English, as in "The Decalogue is another name for the
---- Commandments," or "A monocle is a lens for use
in only ---- eye." The student can then complete familiar
and later unfamiliar expressions by substituting the
Greek prefixes (which may be present on a panel during
early stages) as in "The five-sided building in Washington
used by the Army is called the -------gon," or "People
who make a practice of having only one wife or husband
are called ---------gamous," or "A line of poetry having
six feet is called ------meter." From such general
material the student can then be transferred to a specific
application--as in being asked to compose the technical
names for chemical compounds indicated with symbols
("CF_4 is carbon ----------fluoride") or to write the

symbols for compounds named, "Osmium octafluoride is written-------." The ultimate goal is to permit the student to move quickly from a numerical aspect of a non-verbal stimulus or from a numerical verbal stimulus to a verbal response containing the Greek prefix.

Much of learning a new language is of this nature.

References

1. Skinner, B. F., Verbal Behavior. New York: Appleton-Century-Crofts, 1957.

5

James G. Holland

Harvard University

A TEACHING MACHINE PROGRAM

IN PSYCHOLOGY

A program was written for approximately one quarter of a course in Behavioral Science. The program covered material similar to that covered by about 200 pages of the text (<u>Science and Human Behavior</u>). This required 48 sets of "lessons," each usually containing 29 frames or "items." The students who took the course were 187 Harvard and Radcliffe students, primarily sophomores but including many juniors and seniors and a few freshmen and graduate students. The median time to complete a disk was 18 minutes, or a total of approximately 14.5 hours for the median student to complete the program. When all machine work was completed the students were required to fill out a questionnaire. They reported rather favorable impressions of the machine work. For example in answering the item: "When I read <u>Science and Human Behavior</u>, after working through relevant material on the machine, I felt that the machine," 1% of the respondents checked "contributed nothing," 37% checked "was of some help," and 62% checked "made the text much easier to understand."

An analysis of performance on a final examination given on the lecture and outside reading showed that items for which the machine would have been expected to be of help were much more frequently answered correctly than items for which the machine work was irrelevant.

69

The paper describes in detail the programming techniques used. These techniques have evolved over several years through attempts of various persons to program a variety of subject matters. The subject matter was ordered so as to provide a gradual progression with a minimum of errors. Lists of terms and examples were carefully prepared to assure the student would be made able to converse about the subject matter in as wide a context as possible. Techniques for getting out new or low strength responses with a minimum of errors included (a) the use of panels (short passages of printed material, graphs, etc.) in front of the student while working on a particular set, (b) use of new words in a series of frames before requiring the student to use them, (c) moving from definitions to examples within a single frame, (d) "leading-in" from an assumed common knowledge, (e) indicating relevant categories to which the response term belongs, (f) using high-association words or common phrases, (g) eliminating undesired alternative responses by careful phrasing of the frames. The strengths and deficiencies of this program are revealed by an item analysis of the students' responses.

Editor's Note

Dr. Holland went on to describe a section of the course taught at Harvard University that used ten teaching machines. Students who enrolled in the course received credit upon completion of the material. The following are examples from the machine program. The term "disk" refers to the sets of items that were part of the machine program. A "panel" was text material which accompanied certain disks. It was expected that the student would refer to the panel while working on the disk.

Note: The underlined words or phrases are the correct answers. The percentage in parentheses to the right indicates the proportion of students who gave this answer.. The nonunderlined answers are incorrect.

Disk No. 8

1. Performing animals are sometimes trained with rewards. A hungry animal can be rewarded with food (98%).

2. The trainer rewards the animal for a good performance by giving it food when (13%), or if (14%), after (59%), providing (5%), it has performed correctly.

3. Reward and performance occur in the temporal order: (1) performance (97%), (2) reward (97%).

4. Food given to a hungry animal is not a reward for a response unless it is given at the right time, just after performing (74%).

5. The reward does not act as a stimulus to elicit (75%), condition (14%) the response.

6. A reward simply makes it more probable (34%) or likely (45%) certain (20%), that an animal will behave in the same way again.

7. Food is probably not rewarding if the animal is not deprived of food (0%), or hungry (94%).

8. If an animal is not rewarded for a response, future responses will become less probable or common (28%), likely (22%), frequent (23%), intense, etc. (14%).

9. To make sure an animal will perform at the right time, the trainer rewards (54%), reinforces (9%), conditions (14%), elicits (18%), the behavior frequently.

10. A hungry pigeon in the park flicks dead leaves about with quick movements of its beak. It is rewarded (88%),

reinforced (4%), conditioned (3%), for this behavior
whenever it uncovers bits of food.

11. A pigeon is occasionally rewarded for flicking leaves
about because of the common natural spatial relation of
leaves over food (81%), some specific food (14%).

12. The rewards used by animal trainers are deliberately
arranged; the arrangement of leaves and food in the park,
however, is natural (23%) or nondeliberate (14%), acci-
dental, random, etc. (60%).

13. A technical term for reward is reinforcement. To
reward an organism with food is to reinforce (100%) it
with food.

14. Technically speaking, a thirsty organism can be
reinforced (90%), NOTE NOT REWARDED, rewarded (7%),
with water.

15. In order for food to be reinforcing, the animal must
first be without (10%), or deprived of (73%), lacking, etc.
(11%), food for some time.

16. Reinforcing a response produces an increase in the
probability (87%), or likelihood (9%), chances (3%), that
the response will occur again.

17. We do not observe probability directly. We say that
a response has become more probable if it is observed
more frequently (43%), or often (40%), closely or directly
(9%), under controlled conditions.

18. Technically speaking, to get an animal to respond more
frequently we reinforce (88%), condition (9%), the response.

19. In laboratory research various devices are used to
reinforce behavior. Heat can be used to reinforce (92%),
reward (2%), condition (3%), the behavior of a cold animal.

20. An electrically operated food magazine which presents food can be used to reinforce (97%), condition (2%), reward (1%), the behavior of an organism deprived of food.

21. If the cold (or food-deprived) organism turns on an electrically operated heat lamp (or food magazine), this behavior will be reinforced (87%).

22. The behavior of turning on the electrically operated heat lamp or food magazine will occur more frequently (59%), or often (34%) in the near future if the organism is cold or hungry.

23. In a typical apparatus the depression of a horizontal bar automatically operates the food magazine. The apparatus selects "bar pressing" as the response (49%), or behavior (27%), performance, action, etc. (9%), to be reinforced.

24. The response of pressing a bar must occur at least once in order to be reinforced (93%), conditioned (4%).

25. If pressing the bar does not operate the food magazine, the response is not reinforced (99%), conditioned (1%).

26. Reinforcement makes responses more frequent, while failure to receive reinforcement makes responses less frequent (73%), etc. (12%).

Panel for Disk No. 9

(This description was in front of the student while he used Disk No. 9).

A "hungry" pigeon is placed in a standard experimental space, which consists of an enclosed rectangular chamber or box. Eliciting stimuli, which always precede reflex behavior, are absent; nevertheless, the pigeon may

eventually peck the small disc-shaped key. The food
magazine operates automatically making food available
immediately after any peck (response) on the key. We
observe that the pigeon pecks, receives food, soon pecks
again, receives food, and pecks again, etc. , (i. e. , rate
or frequency of pecking has increased). Since the rate
increases when followed by food, food is said to reinforce
the response, and food is called a reinforcer. Because
the response appears to lack any eliciting stimulus, the
response is said to be emitted. This type of behavior,
which operates or acts upon the environment, is called
operant behavior. [1]

     If, after the key pecking operant is conditioned, the
pigeon never receives food when it pecks, the behavior
of pecking extinguishes (i. e. , the rate of emitting responses decreases until it reaches the low rate which
prevailed before conditioning).

NEW TECHNICAL WORDS

response

operant

respondent

probability

---

[1] When referring to the behavior generally rather than
to specific instances of it, we use the term operant, e. g. ,
key pecking is an operant; but for specific instances we use
the term response; e. g., a peck on the key is a response.
(Reflex behavior, which we have already studied is
also called respondent behavior. This behavior occurs
only in response to eliciting stimuli.

rate (frequency)

emit

reinforcement, reinforcing stimulus, (reinforce)

extinction

Disk No. 9

1. When a pgieon if first placed in the experimental space described, there is a low <u>probability</u> (96%), chance (3%), that it will soon peck the key.

2. To say that a pigeon shows at first a low probability of pecking the key means it will peck at a low <u>rate</u> or <u>frequency</u>, (80% gave both answers), (17% gave only one answer).

3. Eventually the pigeon may <u>emit</u> (81%), reinforce (6%), elicit (4%), the response of pecking the key. (USE TECHNICAL TERM).

4. A given peck on the key is a(n) (1) <u>response</u> (93%). The behavior of "pecking a key" is a(n) (2) <u>operant</u> (90%), response (3%).

5. When the first peck is <u>reinforced</u> (95%), rewarded (2%), paired, followed (3%), with food, the probability of another peck is increased.

6. When pecking the key is followed immediately with food, the <u>rate</u> (51%) or <u>frequency</u> (32%), probability (7%), operant, response (10%), of pecking is observed to increase.

7. The temporal order of the response and the reinforcing stimulus is first (1) <u>response</u> (87%), or <u>pecking</u> (7%), reinforcing (55%), then (2)

reinforcement (18%), or receiving food (7%), stimulus (9%).

8. A stimulus elicits a response in (1) respondent, or reflex behavior. The temporal order is first the (2) stimulus then the (3) response. All three correct (72%).

9. Some would say "the pigeon has acquired a habit of pecking the key," but the only thing observed is an increased rate (59%) or frequency (32%), response, etc. (6%), probability (3%).

10. When food no longer follows the pecking, the (1) rate (67%) or frequency (22%) of emitting the response gradually declines. This process is called (2) extinction (97%), behavior, etc. (3%).

11. When the rate of pecking has returned to its initial low level as a result of withholding food, the operant is said to be extinguished (67%), extinct (24%).

12. In the panel experiment the pecking response slightly moves the key. In general an operant acts upon, or changes, affects (84%) the environment.

13. The diameters of visceral organs are changed by (1) smooth (96%) muscles. Parts of the skeletal frame are moved by (2) striate (90%), striped (4%), skeletal (2%), muscles.

14. Action upon the environment usually results from movement of the skeletal frame. Operants are usually contractions of striate (93%), smooth (3%), skeletal, striped (4%), muscles.

15. A hungry infant cries and is fed; soon the baby cries regularly when hungry. Feeding is said to have reinforced (72% elicited (5%), conditioned (14%), emitted (5%), crying.

16. A psychologist fed her infant son when he emitted a
faint "cooing" sound. The rate (57%) or frequency (25%),
probability (6%), response, etc. (10%), of emitting
"cooing" responses when hungry increased as a result
of this reinforcement.

17. The psychologist fed her son when he emitted "coos"
but not when he cried. Crying when hungry (1) extinguished (88%), decreased (11%) because of the withholding of (2) reinforcement (92%), food (3%), (USE
TECHNICAL TERMS).

18. Vocalizations are (1) operants (79%) because they
act upon the (social) environment, and their frequency
depends on whether or not they are (2) reinforced (96%),
emitted (10%).

19. When you are thirsty, it is very (1) probable (82%),
or likely (16%) that you will walk to a water fountain because such behavior has been (2) reinforced (89%),
conditioned (5%), in the past.

20. If a water fountain consistently fails to operate, you
cease to go to it when thirsty. Because of the lack of
(1) reinforcement (96%) the operant has (2) extinguished (97%).

21. If pecking a key briefly turns off a very loud noise,
frequency of pecking in the presence of the noise will be
observed to increase. The termination of the noise has
served to reinforce (77%), extinguish (13%), emit (6%),
an operant.

22. Reinforcement which consists of presenting stimuli
(e. g. , food or water) is called positive reinforcement.
As one might expect, reinforcement which consists of
terminating stimuli (e. g. , loud noise or painful
stimuli) is called negative (96%), aversive (2%),
positive (1%), reinforcement.

23. A child has a "temper tantrum" screaming for candy.
The mother gives the child the candy, and the tantrum
ceases. The mother's response of handing the candy to
the child is (1) reinforced, elicited (19%) by the (2) termination, stimulus (19%) (both correct 56%), of the
tantrum.

24. If the termination of a "temper tantrum" reinforces
a mother's response of handing candy to her child, this
is an example of negative (77%), positive (16%), operant
(3%), reinforcement.

25. When a "temper tantrum" results in the receipt of
candy, the probability increases that the child will (1) emit
(57%), repeat, etc. (17%), increase (8%), the response
in the near future. In this example, the "temper tantrum"
is technically said to be (2) positively (78%), negatively
(14%), reinforced.

26. To avoid conditioning "temper tantrums" the mother
should not (1) reinforce such behavior. If the behavior
has been previously conditioned, she can (2) extinguish
it by consistently not (3) reinforcing it. (All three
correct 91%).

27. In the vernacular a man is said to have a "tendency"
to listen to music or an "interest" in music. This means
only that he frequently (57%), or often (10%), consistently
(7%), probably (8%), emits the behavior of listening to
music.

Disk No. 10

(The panel was not used while working with this disk.)

1. A stimulus which follows a response is called (1) reinforcing (23%), if the (2) frequency, or rate (89%) of similar responses is observed to increase.

2. Positive reinforcement consists of the presentation
(45%), reinforcement (28%), operant (12%), of stimuli.

3. Negative reinforcement consists of the termination
(20%), removing, ending (42%), of stimuli.

4. Turning off a television commercial is reinforced by
a(n) (1) negative (98%), reinforcer; turning on a very
funny program is reinforced by a(n) (2) positive (98%)
reinforcer.

5. A man turns his face away from an ugly sight. Turning is a(n) (1) response (83%), operant (8%), which is
reinforced by (2) terminating (53%), dislike of (12%),
the ugly sight.

6. A food-deprived child will probably ask for food if
the (1) operant (16%), response (75%), "asking for food"
has been (2) reinforced (100%), in the past. This is an
example of (3) positive (96%) reinforcement.

7. Absenteeism increases if employees are not sufficiently reinforced (96%), with wages and suitable working
conditions.

8. When an infant emits the sounds "da-da" his father
fondles him. We classify fondling as a reinforcer when
we note that the infant (1) emits (86%) "da-da" more
(2) frequently (81%), often (18%).

9. "What does he see in her " means "How does she
reinforce (87%), respond to (4%) his courting behavior
(USE TECHNICAL TERM)?

10. The man who brings candy to his wife to end an argument may find later that his wife argues (1) more frequently, more often. If so, he may suspect that candy
is a (2) reinforcer (both correct 70%).

11. The man who brings his wife candy when she is especially agreeable may find that she argues (1) less frequently, or less often (91%). He has (2) reinforced (63%), conditioned (8%), elicited (10%), responses which are incompatible with arguing.

12. If people continue to emit the behavior of buying books, music, and works of art, we may conclude that these are reinforcers (22%), or reinforcing (15%), reinforcements (12%), reinforced (34%).

13. In operant conditioning a response can only be reinforced after it has been emitted (73%), performed, etc. (9%).

14. If a school teacher dismisses a class when the students are rowdy, she will probably do so again because she is (1) reinforced (79%), conditioned (7%), by (2) termination (84%), ending (5%), of the stimuli arising from a rowdy class.

15. The teacher who dismisses a class when it is rowdy (1) increases (89%), reinforces (7%), the probability of future rowdy behavior, since dismissal from class is probably a (2) reinforcer (39%), reinforcement (57%) for rowdy children.

16. The teacher who dismisses the class when they are quiet (1) decreases (87%) the probability of rowdy behavior. She is conditioning (2) responses (51%), or behavior (25%), operants (4%) incompatible with rowdiness.

17. If we consistently get no answer when we dial a number we stop dialing. This process is called (1) extinction (87%). The change is due to lack of (2) reinforcement (90%), reinforcers (4%).

18. If an airplane spotter never sees the kind of plane he is to spot, he looks at the sky (1) less frequently or

at a lower rate. In other words his "looking" behavior
(2) extinguishes (both correct 77%).

19. A pigeon pecks a key and immediately receives food.
Food is a(n) (1) reinforcement (43%), reinforcer (53%),
for the response. After this it is more (2) probable
(75%) or likely (19%) that the pigeon will again peck
the key.

20. When a pigeon is reinforced for pecking a key the
(1) rate, or frequency (95%) at which the response is
(2) emitted (89%), increases.

21. If a previously reinforced response is no longer reinforced, it soon occurs (1) less frequently (83%). This
is called (2) extinction (97%).

22. To stop a dog from begging for food one should
extinguish (83%) the operant by never again feeding him
when he begs.

23. Reaching for a glass of water or saying "water,
please" is a(n) (1) operant; any specific instance of such
behavior, however, is called a(n) (2) response (both
correct 71%; answers reversed 14%).

24. After a response has been reinforced, the probability
(95%) is high that it will be repeated again.

25. There is no eliciting stimulus for a(n) (1) operant
(91%); there is an eliciting stimulus for a(n) (2) respondent (28%), reflex (30%), response (29%).

26. (1) Operant (88%) behavior usually acts upon the external environment; (2) respondent (74%), behavior usually
affects the internal economy of the organism.

27. Most (1) respondent (91%), reflex (1%), internal
(2%), behavior involves the activity of smooth muscles

and glands.   Most (2) <u>operant</u> (91%),   external (2%),
behavior involves the activity of striate muscles.

28.   In looking for lost car keys, one may search the
same table top several times before this behavior
<u>extinguishes</u> (94%), terminates, etc. (3%).

6

Susan R. Meyer
Harvard University

A PROGRAM

IN ELEMENTARY ARITHMETIC:

PRESENT AND FUTURE

The machine designed by IBM to teach elementary arithmetic and spelling made its debut in a school late in October (1958). The initial test was designed only to indicate areas of difficulty that might arise in the operation of a complicated mechanism by children of various sizes and levels of scholastic ability. The period of testing also provided an opportunity to test certain sections of the extended arithmetic program that has been constructed for eventual use with a battery of the machines. The test of the program was, to say the least, "dirty"-- failure of a child to grasp a point could be blamed on the faulty preparation in arithmetic provided by the less-than-perfect school system. A description of the program, spiced with the behavioral "comments" of the first subjects will be the main topic of this paper.

In designing the program, three questions had to be answered: (1) what relevant behavior must be assumed to be available, (2) what behavior constitutes competence in arithmetic, and (3) what is the best order of steps from the starting point to the final competence?

1. The behavior assumed to be available in the present program includes a level of discrimination requisite to matching a letter or number with its equivalent on the answer slider. Interpretation of pictures representing objects and actions, and a minimal reading

83

vocabulary ("is, " "here, " "and, " etc.) is an integral part of the method of presentation, and non-readers would probably be ruled out.

2. Arithmetic teachers agree that "meaningful" use of the arithmetic operations is as important as accuracy. The program develops many ways of "looking at" and "talking about" the operations as well as teaching the responses to the standard representations of arithmetic "facts. "

3. The "course" begins with the numbers 0, 1, and 2, followed by the introduction of the concept of addition as a process of putting groups together and as steps up a number series. The other single digit numbers are introduced as one more than the preceding number, with subtraction following 3, multiplication following 4, and division following 6. By the time the student learns the number 9, he has been led through all the possible groupings of the digits not involving larger numbers. He has had to respond to an extensive vocabulary and many different pictorial representations, and has learned to fill in any missing component in an arithmetic "sentence, " including simple numerical equations. Data from students who have been exposed to arithmetic for 1-5 years support the assumption made in designing the program that knowing "1 + 1 is?" does not mean knowing that "2 is 1 +? " or "1 +? is 2. " According to the texts for teachers of arithmetic, there are only 100 or so "facts" with answers less than 10, but recent experience with children acquiring bits of this repertoire indicates that the more than two thousand responses required by the present program may be too few.

7

Douglas Porter
Harvard University

SOME EFFECTS

OF YEAR LONG TEACHING

MACHINE INSTRUCTION

Throughout the academic year 1957-58 an experiment was carried out in the teaching of spelling to elementary school children. This study, under sponsorship of the United States Office of Education, is exploratory in nature and not expected to give definitive answers to the many problems of programming and presenting learning materials via teaching machine. The great mass of student response data has not yet been completely analyzed, but more conventional testing provides some suggestive results.

Teaching machines of maximum simplicity were used for economic and mechanical reasons. Teaching materials printed on conventional 8-1/2 x 11 sheets are fed past two windows in the machine by means of a unidirectional friction-drive roller. Student responses are written directly on the teaching materials through the lower window. Operation of a lever moves the written response to the upper window, under glass, and exposes the correct response in the lower window. The student compares his answer and then scores himself right or wrong. The operating lever is again moved, bringing up the next item. Sole mechanical functions of the machine are to provide immediate response confirmation, prevent cheating, and keep subjects from having access to any but the current teaching item.

85

Teaching materials were prepared to parallel as closely as possible the standard lesson materials used by the control groups and prescribed by the school. Actual words taught were exactly the same, and sentence contexts and reading difficulty of the materials were carefully matched. Within the above limitations teaching machine materials were programmed to require the following sequence of response: identification of the spelling words in a meaningful sentence context; matching the correct word to a given definition; matching several words on the basis of letter structure; and writing missing letters in words presented in a sentence context. No spoken instruction was given. The following is a sample of the program material:

1. Underline these words: thunder, steady, soaked, frightened

   I hadn't gone half way when thunder rolled and rain came down in a steady pour. I was soaked. I made a dash for an old horse shed. And there was Wolf. Crouching in the shadow, he looked so like a wolf that for a moment he frightened me.

   frightened   steady   thunder soaked

2. Circle the word that rhymes with ready: thunder steady pour soaked
      steady

3. Circle the word that means firm, regular, or not shaking:

   steady thunder umbrella southern sweeping

   steady

4. Write the missing letters:

   Then rain came down in a s_____ea__y
   pour.

   steady

5. Write the missing letters; they are all
   the same:

   Ragged clouds were sw___ ___ping the
   south___rn sky.

   southern   sweeping

6. Write the missing letters:

   Without thinking of an umbre___ ___a, I
   set out.

   umbrella

7. Write the missing letters:

   Halfway to the store thu___ ___er rolled.

   thunder

8. Write the missing letters:
   Then rain came down in a s__ea__y pour.
   steady

9. Write the missing letters:

   Brushing, moving quickly, s__ee__ing.

   sweeping

Twenty-two out of the normal 34 weeks of spelling instruction were given on both the sixth and second grade levels via teaching machine, and student achievement compared to control groups taught in a more usual specified manner. Subsidiary information was gathered on student achievement in other areas, intelligence scores, student reaction to teaching machine instruction, sex differences in achievement, amount of time spent in teaching machine instruction, change in student performance throughout the year, number and type of errors made in responding to teaching program, and transfer of training to concomitant written materials and spelling words not specifically taught.

Some of the experimental findings follow (statistical results are to be found in the table below).

Sixth Grade Data

1. Mean student achievement over the year in "grade equivalent" scores:　　Experimental group 1. 42
    　　　　　　　　　　　　　　　　Control group　　　0. 90
    　　　　　　　　　　　　　　　　　　(sign test, 0. 01)

2. Mean student achievement within experimental group: Machine lessons　97. 2%
    　　　　　　　　　　　　　　　　Book lessons　　　96. 4%
    　　　　　　　　　　　　　　　　　(sign test, 0. 025)
    　　　　　　　　　　　　　　(gain of 1. 2 words/week)

3. First vs second half of machine taught lessons: no significant difference.

4. "Time at study" ratio: E/C = 1/3.

5. Miscellaneous correlations (rho):

    I. Q. vs Achievement in: Experimental group -0. 128 (n. s.
    　　　　　　　　　　　　Control group　+0. 343 ($<$ 0. 05)

Sex of student vs achievement   (n. s.)
Liking of machine instruction vs   (n. s.)
achievement
Errors per response vs   (n. s.)
achievement

6. Preference for spelling instruction: with machines 17
                                         teacher   12
                                         no difference   2

Second Grade Data

1. Mean student achievement over the year:

In "grade equivalent" scores: Experimental group 0. 80
                               Control group   1. 10
                               (U test, 0. 005)

In letter-position scores: Experimental group 65. 6
                               Control group   37. 8
                               (U test, 0. 001)

2. Ad libitum lesson spread:

In four weeks' time   9 lessons
In twelve weeks' time 9 lessons

On both second and sixth grade levels spelling achievement as measured by standardized achievement tests was significantly superior for the experimental groups, and there is essentially no relationship between intelligence scores and achievement in the experimental groups, but a significant positive relationship in the control groups. There is no relationship in either group between sex of students or liking of instructional method and achievement. As a rough indication of student motivation throughout the year--it might be expected that the

"novelty" of a new instructional process would wear off--
weekly test scores for the first and second half of the
machine lessons were compared with no differences apparent. Within the sixth grade experimental group,
there is a positive relationship between the number of
responses per lesson required of subjects and consequent
achievement, but no relationship between the number of
errors per lesson and achievement.

Several observations were made concerning
general efficiency of the teaching machine process of
instruction. In the sixth grade, lesson materials were
available on the usual week-by-week basis, but the experimental group spent about one-quarter as much time
studying as the control group. In the second grade, lesson materials were available on an ad libitum basis for
12 weeks, during which time the spread of materials
being worked on by students extended to nine lessons.
These high rates of responding are due in part to the
release of better students from the usual constraints of
group study, but in addition, the machines and/or program seems to generate rapid responding.

8

Donald E. P. Smith
University of Michigan

SPECULATIONS:

CHARACTERISTICS OF SUCCESSFUL

PROGRAMS AND PROGRAMMERS

Since the technique of programming materials for teaching machines is still in swaddling clothes, a report of hunches may be appropriate. Some principles and techniques were prepared to guide text-book authors who wish to make the transition from text material to machine programming. Further ideas on programming have derived from recent experience in editing and field testing a program on English grammar. The program, written by Mr. Joseph Blumenthal at the request of Harcourt, Brace and Co., Inc., was designed for use in the ninth grade. It consists of some two thousand frames.

Programming

1. One index of the success of a program may be the proportion of correct responses emitted by the learner. Other things equal, learning varies directly with the proportion of correct responses according to Skinner's position. Such a statement assumes that each frame or task requires a response which contributes to the desired final behavior. The present program, tested on thirty seventh grade slow learners (range of I. Q. scores: 75-90), produced 91% correct responses.

2. On the other hand, there may be some advantage to inducing some errors. Apparently, in an imperfect program, motivation runs high, so much so

that even "honest" children try to cheat. It seems as
though the possibility of failure enhances the reinforcing
effect of a successful response. Thus failure on some
items may contribute to the effectiveness of the learning.

3. The question is often raised concerning the
appropriateness of a given program for the bright and
the dull. The bright can easily skip steps and still
understand. The dull probably require many more steps
or frames than do the bright. Should the bright be required to use the same program as the dull?

The answer may be as follows: while the bright
can skip steps and still understand, it may be salutary
to require that they take every step anyway. As a result,
they should be better able to retrace their conceptual
paths when necessary.

The problem of the dull appears to be retention.
Frequent reviews are required of them while the bright
seem to require few or none. Retention appears to be
especially difficult under two conditions: (1) when the
learner is chronically anxious; and (2) when the material
to be learned is of the "nonsense" kind, e. g. , spelling,
foreign language, and technical terminology in which the
name of the term bears no obvious relationship to the
process for which it stands (e. g. , "conditioning" as
contrasted with "extinction"). Since a conditioning procedure is used, nonsense material is relatively easy to
program. Unfortunately, it may not be so easily retained by anxious students.

Programmers

One of the most striking similarities among the successful programmers with whom I have worked is an inverted
style of thinking. The inverted thinker focusses so intensively upon a stimulus configuration, either perceptual

or conceptual, that the differentiation process appears to continue far beyond that of the normal. Such a person tends to be analytical, deductive, methodical, perfectionistic--in short, the classical or Jungian introvert. In thinking style, he is diametrically opposite to the extravert who tends to skim over the conceptual surface of life, to think elliptically, synthetically, inductively. Coincident with the inverted thinking is a willingness to continue a task long after the normal (and especially the extravert) has reached the point of satiation.

After the program has been field-tested and an error analysis begun, a different kind of thinking may be required. Many errors seem so nonsensical or arbitrary that a discursive or imaginative style of thinking may be useful for discovering their origin. For example, the responses of introverts on a word association test tend to be highly predictable (boy-girl) while the extravert's response is largely unpredictable (boy-money: i. e. , boy- [Greenlease kidnapping - ransom] -money). It may take such a discursive style of thinking to induce the conceptual trails followed by students when they emit an unexpected response. In other words, the extravert may be able to reconstruct unusual patterns of thinking by starting only with an error. Next, the blind alleys can be blocked off by preemptive words, reduction of extraneous stimuli, and by the use of prompts.

Selection of personnel for writing programs may well be facilitated by using a measure of extraversion-introversion.

Principles of Programming

I. Define precisely the desired behavior and the form or forms which it must take:

e. g. To recognize the parts of speech--

    a.   To name the nouns in a sentence.

    b.   To name the verbs in a sentence.

    Etc.

To recognize the parts of a sentence--

    a.   To recognize the subject--

       i.   To name the complete subject.

       ii.   To name the noun portion of the subject.

       iii.   To name verb forms used as a subject (gerund, participle).

       iv.   To identify the referent of a pronoun used as the subject.

       v.   To specify the number of the subject as implied by the verb.

    b.   To recognize the predicate--

    Etc.

II.   Determine the steps to be learned which, when summated, will comprise the behavior:

  e. g. a.   Learn words which are nouns.

        b.   Learn the difference between a noun and a verb.

        c.   Learn to call a noun by its technical name.

        Etc.

III. Introduce the concept, the operation of the relationship between concept and operation. Define all
terms to be used. (E. g. , term, number, right
side, word, etc.)

Methods:

A. Introduction by definition:

1. In this case, use a common sense definition
without technical words:

e. g. , A noun is the name of something.

2. Follow in the same frame with an example,
part of which S can formulate:

e. g. , "Tim" is a noun because it is the
_____ of a boy.

3. Follow, in another frame, with an example
requiring S to use the technical word (or,
if the word is not likely to be remembered,
give more examples in which the term is
exposed before calling for it).

e. g. , "Sue" is a _____ because it is the
_____ of a girl.

4. Introduce contrast. Show what the concept
is not, and point out concepts, easily confused, which are not the same as the focal
concept:

a. "Because" is not a _____ because it is
_____ the name of something.

b. "He is a fine fellow. "

Fellow is a _____ but he is not a noun.

because it is <u>not</u> the _____ of
something.

5. Use transitional contrast words to alert S
    to contrast (<u>e. g.</u>, but, on the other hand, etc.).

B. Introduction by example:

 <u>e. g.</u>, Boy, girl, hat, dog, house--all these are
    names of things. They are called nouns.
    The name, <u>tree</u>, is called a _____.

C. Introduction by anticipation:

 The subject is a noun (and sometimes a
    verb form called a gerund) which does
    something.
    In "Birds fly, " the subject is _____.

 Including the term, gerund, as an irrelevancy
in several preceding items seems to sensitize
S so that he can be prompted into the correct
response.

 <u>e. g.</u>, One verb form used as a noun is called
a g-----.

D. Introduction by prompts:

 The prompt is a technique for causing emission
of a response which might not normally be made.
To illustrate, in the example above, "g-----"
is a mechanical prompt. In a sense, the whole
Socratic method consists of a series of prompts,
in question form. That is, each question acts
as a signpost at a fork, leading S along a specific path of reasoning. However, the term
"prompt" is usually reserved for simple

verbal techniques which elicit desired responses. They are enumerated in V below.

IV. The web of learning

Once the concept of operation has been introduced, it is necessary to build a web of learning. The web is provided by tying the new to the old, by providing as many synonyms and antonyms for the concept as possible, by progressing from concrete illustration to abstract definition and back again, and by repetition and spaced reviews.

Basic to the task is a process and a product. The process is formulation of the answer to questions, the product is understanding (rather than rote learning). The learner should know why and how he has trod certain pathways so that, if parts are forgotten, they can be reconstructed.

Methods may be categorized as those involving repetition and those involving developmental sequences.

A. Repetition:

1. Pure repetition:

a. Practice of the response. Once the technical term has been emitted, the following frames should require that it continue to be emitted, first alone and then in combination with other technical terms. For example, "non-reinforcement" and "extinction" need to be used together since one is a consequence of the other. (As a result of the practice, the term and its associates become easier and

easier to arouse, thus requiring
less work by S).

2. Repetition by variation:

   a. Similarities and Contrasts. Many
     examples should be used, some of
     them illustrating the dimensions in
     which the concept operates and others
     illustrating what the concept is <u>not.</u>

     The grammatical structure, if it
     is irrelevant to the concept, must be
     varied so that it will cancel out.

     In general, if there are several
     ways to say the same thing, use
     them all. <u>Redundacy is required.</u>

B. Developmental Sequences

1. Known to unknown. Begin with a common
experience which illustrates the concept.
Expose the part of.that experience which
relates to the concept. Then attach the
technical term to the common term.

     e. g. The child likes candy. He will
     smile when he sees candy. Giving him
     the candy for smiling constitutes a re-
     ward. A technical term similar to re-
     ward is reinforcement.

2. Concrete to abstract. To illustrate
number concepts, we commonly
start with objects, then pictures
of objects, then numbers, then
algebraic terms.

.e. g. ,   1.   000 = ⓪①②③

2. $3 = \dfrac{6}{2}$

3.   a = 2b

3. Common experience, to technical description of stimuli and responses in
experience, to application of technical
terms in new situations.

e. g. , Using the candy example, go
from candy to secondary reinforcements
like the smiling of a parent then back to
Eisenhower's smile.

V. Prompts

A. Similarity:

1. Of ideas:

"Just as the smoke from a fire rises,
warm air when heated will _____."

2. Of signals:
"Naturally" signals a common sense
answer.

"a + b = b + a is the associative law
for addition.
Then, naturally, a x b = b x a is the
associative law for _____."

3. Of grammatical construction:

"The hotter, the faster the molecules move.
The colder, the ____ the molecules move."

B. Contrast:

    1. Of Ideas: "Warm air rises; cold air
                  _____."

    2. Of Signals: "+ 6 is greater than -1 and +3
                  is greater than -2 but -6 is
                         _____ than -2.

C. Grammatical construction:

    Some constructions limit the range of
    response.

        e. g.   "The word candy sometimes comes
              just _____ candy is put in the mouth. "

    (a temporal word like before or
    after is required.)

D. Echoic devices:

    A tendency for perseveration can be used
    to elicit a response.

    "If food always follows a response, the
    subject is _____ reinforced. "

E. The whole:

    When a rule or principle is stated in simple
    terms, the steps leading to the rule can be
    answered by reference to the sense of the whole.

        e. g.   "The first time a child has candy in
              his mouth, the _____ elicits salivation;
              thus the salivation reflex is unlearned. "

Step 1.

"The word 'candy' will make a child's mouth water only after some _____ ."

F. Hints:

When a problem requires use of earlier learnings, reference to those learnings may be used.

G. Mechanical Devices:

First letter of the answer; number of letters in the answer indicated by dashes; color or size of type may be varied (e. g. , caps for unconditioned stimulus and response, small letters for conditioned).

VI. Vanishing or Cue Reduction

On repeated material, reduce cues as follows:

"Birds fly. " The word "birds" _____ a noun.
"Monkeys climb. " The _____ "monkeys" is a noun.
"Boys fight. " The word _____ is a noun.
"Girls giggle. " The word "girls" is a _____ .
"Birds fly. " The word _____ is a _____ .

VII. Summation

After all the concepts and operations are learned, put them all into a problem so that they will constitute a whole (be integrated).

VIII. Review

In general, the more the repetition that is required for learning, the more frequent the reviews which

must be given.   These should be immediate (every
five or ten frames) and delayed (every twenty to
forty frames).

A.   Don't expect much independent thought of
the learner.   Make the steps so small
that he cannot err.   The error tendency in
programming is toward too few steps
rather than too many.

B.   Stick to one element (concept or operation)
at a time.   Eliminate all irrelevancies
except contrived "anticipators. "

C.   Keep the amount of work (complexity of
recall) very low per reinforcement.

9 Lloyd E. Homme and Robert Glaser

University of Pittsburg

RELATIONSHIPS BETWEEN

THE PROGRAMMED TEXTBOOK

AND TEACHING MACHINES

The teaching device which is being developed at the University of Pittsburgh might be classified as a minor variation on the machine-teaching theme; it can be designated in at least two ways: as a "paper teaching machine" or as a "programmed textbook." The purpose of this paper (1) to make clear what a programmed textbook is, (2) to make a comparison between the programmed textbook's characteristics and the critical requirements of a teaching machine, and, finally, (3) to summarize some preliminary experimentation with the programmed textbook.

The programmed textbook is simple and easily described: its external appearance will not differ from an ordinary textbook, but its interior is quite different. Each page consists of n (usually four or five)panels; the sequence of the panels is not from the top of the page to the bottom as in a conventional textbook; only one panel is "read" or responded to before the student turns the page. The student begins with the top panel on page 1, responds to it, turns to page 2 to get his answer confirmed on the top panel, goes to the top panel of page 3, responds to it, confirms his answer by turning the page, and so on, to the end of the unit or chapter, where he is instructed to return to page 1 and respond to the second panel on each page, and so on to the end of the chapter.

103

Since each panel is numbered, no confusion results in this procedure. It will be noted that the exposure of a series of adjacent panels, a difficulty inherent in most non-mechanical devices, is thus easily circumvented, and that this is accomplished without a masking device of any sort, except the page itself. The fact that the response panel ("answer") of one frame is exposed simultaneously with the stimulus panel ("question") of the succeeding frame has presented no difficulties thus far. As a matter of fact, this characteristic has proved quite convenient (and space-saving); since the exposed response-panel contains an "answer" of only a few words or numbers, the rest of the space on the response panel (as well as, on occasion, the answer itself) can be used as a part of the prompting system for the next frame.

Programmed Textbook Characteristics vis-a-vis the Critical Requirements of Teaching Machines

The main functions of modern teaching machines are (1) to cause the student to emit each response (rather than select one, say, from a group of alternatives), and (2) to lead the student through a large number of steps carefully designed to minimize the probability of incorrect responses. The programmed text is clearly capable of fulfilling these functions since they depend on the structure of the program rather than upon the technique of presenting it. This means that one is faced with the same problems in constructing a program, whether it be for a machine or a programmed textbook. On a more optimistic note, it is a virtual certainty that principles of programming developed for the programmed textbook will be applicable to machine-teaching and vice versa. In fact, there appears to be nothing that would preclude making a program available both as a programmed text, and in the form of disks, cards, or tape for machine use.

The main apparent deficiency of the programmed

text is that it is not equipped with appropriate hardware
to control "cheating. " In Skinner's college teaching
machine, for example, once a disk is locked into the
machine, there is no way in which the student can expose
the machine's answer before he has composed his own.
In the programmed textbook, on the other hand, a student
need only turn the page. However, before the programmed
textbook is condemned on these grounds, there are at
least three points to be made about the cheating that a
hardware machine is designed to prevent.

First, to assert that hardware is essential is
to assert that other means of controlling the subject's
behavior cannot be found; this is something we do not
yet know. Second, we do not really know how damaging
to the learning process this kind of cheating is; the possibility exists that it is not damaging at all. Third, and
most important, is the possibility that with the development of really adequate programming techniques, cheating will occur so infrequently that it will not constitute
a problem of any magnitude. It is quite conceivable
that the tendency to "cheat, " as well as the current widespread insistence upon a "foolproof" hardware machine,
represents nothing more than a vestige of traditional
modes of educational control which will soon be displaced
by other techniques. We may note that a necessary condition for predisposing the behavior we call cheating is
that the tendency to emit the correct response is weak.
Obviously this condition can be avoided in a programmed
sequence. With a well-constructed program in which
non-reinforcement is minimized, pre-exposure of the
answer is also minimized. Further, a well-constructed
sequence is, by definition, a program in which success
on each frame depends on the successful performance
of prior ones; skipping of frames is poorly reinforced
and consequently weak. For these reasons, then, we
have concluded that cheating against the program is not
a problem of vital concern,   and that extensive

instrumentation to circumvent it is not required.

Experience with programmed textbooks appears to support the position that a cheat-proof device is not required with a college population. An additional job which the hardware machine accomplishes is the automatic dropping out of frames to which correct responses have been given. Again, adequate programming which maximizes reinforced responses may largely eliminate the necessity for this contingency but, if not, the function can be simply approximated in the programmed textbook through appropriate instructions.

Some preliminary experimentation with the programmed textbook.

Since the experimentation to be reported upon is described in detail elsewhere (1), it will suffice to summarize it here. Programs were constructed on topics in elementary number theory, statistics, and fundamentals of music. Properties of these programmed learning sequences were manipulated as the independent variable for study. The dependent variable, amount of learning, was measured by conventional written achievement tests of both multiple choice and composed (short answer) types.

To investigate the "size of step" variable, i.e., larger or smaller approximations to desired behavior, four programs, with identical content, consisting of 30, 40, 51, and 67 steps respectively, were constructed on elementary number theory. Independent groups of 5 Ss were assigned to each treatment. Results show that the programs consisting of smaller steps were associated with better immediate test performance, better retention, and fewer errors on the program. The results also indicate the possibility of empirically determining optimal step size. Decreasing step size beyond this point is not required for maximum learning.

Three related experiments were conducted to compare the effectiveness of material presented in conventional textbook form with the same material presented in the programmed textbook. Two of these experiments utilized a sequence written directly from a portion of a standard statistics text, and the third utilized a sequence presenting the fundamentals of music reading. Results show that, in general, the Ss who interacted with the programmed text made higher achievement scores and exhibited less variability of performance than did Ss receiving conventional presentation of the same materials.

The programmed textbook is a simple means for presenting machine-teaching type learning sequences without hardware. The device meets most of the critical requirements of machine teaching, but it cannot prevent cheating. However, it is concluded that, not only is the influence of this variable largely unknown, but it occurs with such infrequency in an adequately constructed program that its importance is likely to be small. Experimentation with several college subject matter programs appears to support the following conclusions: (a) decreasing the "size" of the stimulus-response steps in a program results in better learning and retention, up to a point, and (b) material presented in programmed textbook form results in generally higher and less variable achievement scores on subsequent tests than conventional textbook presentation.

References

1. Evans, J. L. , Glaser, R. , and Homme, L. E. . The effects of variations in the properties of verbal learning sequences of the "teaching machine" type. A paper read at the meetings of the Eastern Psychological Association in April, 1959.

10

Norman A. Crowder
Hoover Electronics Company

AUTOMATIC TUTORING

BY MEANS OF INTRINSIC PROGRAMMING

"Automatic Tutoring" is an individually-used, instructorless method of teaching which represents an automation of the classical process of individual tutoring. The student is given the material to be learned in small logical units (usually a paragraph or less in length) and is tested on each unit immediately. The test result is used automatically to control the material that the student sees next. If the student passes the test question, he is automatically given the next unit of information and the next question. If he fails the question, the preceding unit of information is reviewed, the nature of his error is explained to him and he is retested. The test questions are multiple-choice questions and there is a separate set of correctional materials for each wrong answer that is included in the multiple-choice alternatives.

The structural feature that distinguishes an automatic tutoring device from the type of teaching machine that has been advocated by Professor Skinner and his students is that in an automatic tutoring device the program of instructional material is completely flexible. Each piece of material that the student sees is determined directly by that individual student's immediately precedent behavior in choosing an answer to a multiple-choice question. Since the student's behavior in choosing an answer to the multiple-choice question is determined, presumably, by his state of knowledge at the time he

makes his choice, the automatic tutoring device adapts
the program of material directly to the present state of
knowledge of the individual student.

Evidently any teaching machine which employs
a variable program must incorporate some means of
varying the program on the basis of the student's responses. The method used in the automatic tutoring
materials builds all of the program alternatives into the
programmed material itself in such a way that an elaborate external programming device is unnecessary. The
method is called "intrinsic programming" and is quite
simple. The simplest form of intrinsically programmed
automatic tutoring device is merely a special kind of
book, called a "scrambled book. " The scrambled book
is used as follows: on page 1 of the book the student
finds the first unit of information and the first multiple-
choice question. Each of the alternative answers to the
question is identified by a page number. For example,
the question on page 1 of the scrambled book may look
like this:

> "In the multiplication 3 x 4 = 12, the
> number 12 is called the product and the
> numbers 3 and 4 are called the

>   Page 15   quotients.
>   Page 29   factors.
>   Page 43   powers. "

The student chooses what he believes is the correct
answer to the question and turns to the page number given
in front of that answer. If he has chosen the correct
answer, the page to which he turns will present the next
unit of information or the next concept to be mastered,
and the next question. If he has chosen an incorrect
answer, the page to which he (thereby) turns will explain
why his answer was incorrect, and will direct him to

return to the original choice page to try again. Thus the
student cannot progress through the book except by
eventually choosing the right answer to each question.

The example shown above is the first question
in a scrambled book dealing with the structure of number
systems, and the first topic to be developed in the book
is the basic concept of exponent notation. The point of
the first question is simply to establish whether the
student is familiar with the use of the word "factor."
The correctional material that appears on one of the
wrong answer pages, page 43, reads as follows:

"Page 43

Your answer was: 'powers.'

We'll get to powers of numbers
pretty soon, but we're not there yet.
The numbers that are multiplied together to form a product are called
'factors,' not 'powers.' Now return
to page 1 and choose the right
answer."

The student who has turned to page 43 will now presumably return to page 1, and choose the right answer, "Page
29 factors" and turn to page 29.

The material on the right answer page corresponding to the first question confirms the correctness
of the student's choice and introduces the next topic:

"Page 29

Your answer was: 'factors.'

You are correct. The numbers

which are multiplied together to form a
product are called 'factors.' Thus in the
multiplication '3 x 4 = 12' the numbers
3 and 4 are the factors, 12 is the product.

Is it possible for the same number
(same quantity, that is) to be used as a
factor more than once in forming a
product?

Page 59   Yes
Page 71   No"

The question on page 29 is simply a leading question,
designed to call the student's attention to the fact that
the factors used in forming a product need not necessarily
be different quantities. Should the student for any reason choose the wrong answer, the material he finds
when he (thereby) turns to page 71 will read:

"Page 71

Your answer was: 'No.'

Why not?

In 2 x 2 = 4, 2 occurs as a factor twice.
In 4 x 4 x 4 = 64, 4 occurs as a factor
three times.
In 10 x 10 x 10 x 10 x 10 = 100,000, 10
occurs as a factor five times.

There is nothing in the definition of
multiplication, or of a factor, which pre-
vents the same quantity from occurring
several times as a factor in a multiplication. Now return to page 29 and
choose the right answer."

The material on the right answer page for the question on page 29 reads:

"Page 59

Your answer was: 'Yes.'

Of course it is. For example in the multiplication 4 x 4 x 4 = 64, the number 4 occurs as a factor three times.

What product would you reach by using 2 as a factor 3 times?

Page 81   6
Page 3   8
Page 17   9"

The question on this page should pick up any misunderstandings the student may still have concerning the matter of forming a product by using the same number as a factor several times. When the student has successfully passed this question, the text proceeds to first an informal and then a formal definition of the nth power of a number, x, and so on.

The examples above have been cited at rather tedious length in order first, to explain the mechanics of the method, and second, to call attention to what seems to me to be a fundamental difference in the philosophies underlying automatic tutoring methods and those which underlie the Skinnerian type of teaching machine, at least as the methods have presently developed. If I understand Skinner correctly, he views the teaching machine as a means of setting up a carefully controlled situation in which the student is conditioned to emit appropriate responses to the stimuli presented. Thus for Skinner, the important function of the teaching machine is that it leads the student to emit a response which is progressively brought under the control of the stimuli. The effective learning is evidently considered to be intimately bound up with the process of the student's responding. Skinner therefore quite properly emphasizes that the student's response should be constructed in a free choice situation, rather than recognized in a multiple-choice situation.

I have approached the design of automatic tutoring materials from quite a different point of view. To me, the essential problem is that of controlling a communication process by the use of feedback. The student's response serves primarily as a means of determining whether the communication process has been effective and at the same time allows appropriate corrective action to be taken when the communication has been ineffective. The structural peculiarities of automatic tutoring materials are designed to serve this testing and correctional purpose, and the material is not constrained by any particular theoretical learning model. If an error has occurred, the problem is not solved by revealing the right response to the student, as the failure (of communication) occurred before the response was emitted. What is required, in the case of an error, therefore, is to repeat or revise the communication process. This is what the automatic tutoring materials are designed to do.

The communication process, which I conceive to be the essential process in the teaching of human beings, encompasses a rather wide variety of specific techniques. In any specific instance the question of whether the programmer should employ straight exposition, a leading question, a formal definition followed by examples, a series of examples leading to a formal definition, an analogy, or any of the many other specific techniques of communication needs to be decided on the basis of the specific subject-matter and on what the programmer presently knows of the state of knowledge of the subject. To a very large degree this choice must be made on an arbitrary basis. (If the program is successful, one describes the choices as "intuitive.") The point is that it has seemed to me to be preferable to have all of these communication techniques available, and to employ a check on the success of the communication at each step, rather than attempting to reduce the communication process to a specific conditioning model which does not seem well adapted to the teaching of complex meaningful material.

For research purposes, or for training programs wherein a very close check is desired on the progress of each student, it is convenient to handle the automatic tutoring materials in a special automatic microfilm projector. The automatic microfilm projector in effect turns the pages for the student, that is the student desiring to go to page 127, for example, enters the number 127 into the keyboard of the projector, and the projector automatically searches out and projects the microfilmed page 127. The usefulness of the microfilm device arises primarily from the fact that it can be fitted with a recording mechanism to recover a complete record of the student's progress. Such a device enables one to refine the materials on the basis of experience, and also offers an unprecedented degree of administrative control of an instructional program.

Present experience with automatic tutoring devices has been limited to small-scale laboratory studies. The most striking result of these studies was the excellent acceptance of the material (which was in microfilmed form) by students who were relatively low in verbal skills. The feasibility of preparing material in automatic tutoring form has been demonstrated in such diverse fields as trouble-shooting of complex electronic equipment, law, trigonometry, contract bridge, and

number theory.   The method seems best adapted to
material which can be organized logically and coherently.

The longest program that has been prepared in
automatic tutoring form to date is a 344-page sequence
which covers the principles of positional number systems,
the octal and binary number systems, the conversion of
numbers between systems with different bases, and some
introductory concepts in arithmetic as it is done by electronic computers.   An empirical evaluation of this material in a practical training situation is scheduled for
early 1959.

11

Gustave J. Rath
Nancy S. Anderson
R. C. Brainerd
IBM Research Center

THE IBM RESEARCH CENTER

TEACHING MACHINE PROJECT

Our program of basic psychological research in memory and learning at the IBM Research Center led us toward studying those psychological variables which are important in the design of teaching machines. Thus, we became interested in the general characteristics of teaching machines as opposed to the development of a particular machine.[1] Dr. William J. McGill of Columbia University suggested that the simulation of teaching machines on a high-speed digital computer would be a natural outgrowth of our interest in this field.

The initiation of the project was centered on three basic problems: (1) what subject matter was to be taught, (2) the characteristics of the teaching machine that could be simulated and (3) the vehicle for the simulation. Binary arithmetic was picked as a subject matter to be taught because, in addition to being something that is of interest to the users of high-speed digital computers,

---

[1] The development of a particular machine is being pursued by the IBM Electric Typewriter Division with Dr. B. F. Skinner.

117

it has the feature of containing a small number of new concepts which must be learned, and also has a very small alphabet of characters, namely two. The characteristics of the teaching machine were chosen in a somewhat eclectic and empirical manner within the limitations of the IBM 650 with a typewriter inquiry station. [2] The work of Pressey (5) and of Skinner (7, 8), plus the principles found in psychology texts (3, 4, 9), and in books containing sections of teaching binary arithmetic (2, 6) were used in developing the program of study.

This paper is organized in the following fashion: A description of the philosophy and method of teaching binary arithmetic will be described in detail in the first part. The actual simulation of the teaching machine is described in the second part.

The Teaching of Binary Arithmetic

The Philosophy of Binary Arithmetic

An analysis of the subject matter shows that the concepts of binary arithmetic and decimal arithmetic are the same. Our initial approach consisted of simply defining certain well known arithmetic operations using the binary system and starting as is done in most texts on binary arithmetic. Preliminary experimentation with students from the King's College showed us that the concept of carrying was one of the greatest stumbling blocks in learning binary arithmetic. Thus, we decided that it would be necessary to introduce this concept first, and chose to do this by the method of counting. This approach of teaching arithmetic by counting first is often used in elementary schools for teaching decimal arithmetic.

---

[2]Special input-output devices rather than the usual Inquiry Station Typewriters should be built for this purpose.

When counting, the concept of carrying is used every 10th number in decimal arithmetic but every other number in binary arithmetic. Thus, counting in binary consists of alternately adding 1 and carrying. Furthermore, Addition is nothing more than counting in integer steps equal to or larger than 1, and Subtraction is counting backwards. Multiplication is successive additions with a positional shift each time in the placement of numbers, and Division is successive subtraction with a positional shift.

The Method of Teaching Binary Arithmetic

The "program" for teaching binary arithmetic is basically divided into six parts. Part 1 consists of a counting routine. Here the concept of carrying is taught in the following manner: A student is told to count objects in decimal starting with 0 and he is stopped when he reaches 25. Then he starts again at 95 and is asked to continue counting and is stopped when he reaches 105. He is then told that there are no more 9's in the world. He then is asked to count again, starting with 0, never using a 9 again. He counts as follows: 0 1 2 3 4 5 6 7 8 10 11, up to 25. Then he starts at 85 and counts until 105. If he makes any mistakes, he is taken to the beginning of that set. Once he completes the set, he is told there are no more 8's in the world, and the procedure is then repeated. If he makes no mistakes, he is given the opportunity of skipping 0, 1 or 2 lessons. He then continues counting until eventually he is left with only 0's and 1's with which to count; that is, he is now counting in binary arithmetic up to 10000. This is the end of Part 1.

In Part 2, the student is told to add in the following manner. He is presented the definitions that $0 + 0 = 0$, and $0 + 1 = 1$. Then he is given:

$$0 + 0 = 0$$
$$0 + 1 = 1$$

$$1 + 0 = 1$$
$$1 + 1 = \underline{10}$$
$$10 + 0 = \underline{10}$$
$$0 + 10 = \underline{10}$$
$$10 + 1 = \underline{11}$$
$$1 + 10 = \underline{11}$$
$$10 + 10 = \underline{100}$$
$$0 + 11 = \underline{11}$$

Please note that the underlined numbers indicate that these spaces were to be filled in by the student.

He is then asked to generate what 1 + 1 is. If he makes no mistakes, this procedure is continued until he reaches 11 + 11. If the student makes an error, he is given the same 16 problems in a random order until he does all 16 problems correctly.

The next problems consist of addition of numbers with no carrying, for instance:

$$\begin{array}{r} 1001 \\ + 110 \\ \hline \underline{1111} \end{array}$$

The student is required to do ten correct consecutive problems. If he makes an error on any given problem it is removed and a new problem is presented. Five incorrect problems in a set return him to the previous set.

The next set of problems requires a carry at the far left such as:

$$\begin{array}{r} 10010 \\ + 11101 \\ \hline \underline{101111} \end{array}$$

Now vertical problems are presented:

```
   1
   1
+  1
  11
```

And then to larger problems:

```
   1101
   1001
   1100
+  1000
   1001
 110011
```

Having mastered addition, the student is then taken to Part 3 where he will be taught Subtraction. He is asked to count up to 10000 in binary arithmetic and then asked to start from 10000 and count backwards to 0, which implies subtraction. We continue for all future problems the same error correction rules as were used for addition.

Here the student is first presented the fact that 0 - 0 = 0, and 1 - 0 = 1. He is not presented with the complexity of negative numbers. He then fills out the answers until reaching 11 - 11 in a manner as follows:

```
 0  -  0  =   0
 1  -  0  =   1
 1  -  1  =   0
10  -  0  =  10
10  -  1  =   1
10  - 10  =   0
11  -  0  =  11
11  -  1  =  10
11  - 10  =   1
11  - 11  =   0
```

After having completed the table, he is asked to solve simple subtraction without borrowing as:

$$
\begin{array}{r}
111011 \\
- \ 11001 \\
\hline
\underline{100010} \\
\end{array}
$$

After a set of these problems, he is given a few problems with borrowing only on the last pair of digits on the left such as:

$$
\begin{array}{r}
1011001 \\
- \ 110001 \\
\hline
\underline{101000} \\
\end{array}
$$

After solving a series of problems of this form, he is then presented with multiple borrowing problems. For example:

$$
\begin{array}{r}
1000100 \\
- \ \ 11101 \\
\hline
\underline{100111} \\
\end{array}
$$

After having finished subtraction, the student moves on to Part 4, Multiplication. In Part 4, the simple facts that 1 x 0 = 0, and 1 x 1 = 1 are presented to the student. Then he is given a simple problem such as:

$$
\begin{array}{r}
10 \\
\text{x } 1 \\
\hline
\underline{10} \\
\end{array}
$$

He continues to long multiplication where we present a problem such as:

```
    1101
  x  101
    1101
    0000
   1101
 1000001
```

After having practiced with multiplication, the student is taken into Part 5, Division. Here he is told that he must always work using the long division format. He is reminded that you never divide by 0. He then is presented a sample problem:

```
      10_
   1( 10
```

Followed by a slightly more complicated problem as:

```
       10_
 10 ( 100
```

Now he is given problems with a remainder, such as:

```
         10011
 111 ( 10000101
       111
        10
        00
        101
        000
        1010
         111
         111
         111
```

Once completing division, the student continues to Part 6, which is Conversion. He is first told to count, starting with 0 again, and make columns in binary and decimal, respectively.

Binary	Decimal
0	0
1	1
10	2
11	3
100	4
101	5
110	6
111	7
1000	8

After completing the two columns, the student is asked to repeat the list, using only those numbers which have one 1 in them, and writing the decimal equivalents up to 10000 (binary). He then is asked what is the equivalent of 100000 (binary) in decimal; and if he responds correctly, he is asked for the equivalent of 1000000 (binary) in decimal.

Conversion is taught using the format of an addition problem as shown below. On the left is a binary addition problem, and on the right is its decimal equivalent problem. The student is presented a number on the left such as 1000, and is asked to put its equivalent on the right. Under it, he is given another number, say 100, and asked to put its equivalent on the right. Then he is asked to add the binary numbers and the decimal numbers which shows him how to decompose a binary number. The work sheet is as follows:

Binary	Decimal
1000	8
+ 100	+ 4
1100	12

After finishing a few problems in this dual form, the student is then given a number, such as 1101, and told to find its decimal equivalent by decomposition and addition. After he has mastered this procedure, he is taught conversion from decimal to binary. Here he is asked to perform a series of subtractions on decimal numbers where one always subtracts the largest decimal number of the form 2^N. Then he is asked to write down the binary equivalents of these subtracted numbers and add them together. This demonstrates a method of decimal to binary conversion. Then he works this problem:

Decimal	Binary
72	
-64	1000000
8	
- 8	+ 1000
0	1001000

After completing the six parts of the program, the student is given a final test which is biased toward the problems in which he made the greatest number of mistakes. That is, if he had a great deal of difficulty with multiple carry in addition, but little difficulty in subtraction, he will have more multiple carry problems than subtraction problems.

This completes the course of binary teaching, which we estimate can be done in the mean time of one hour. No real experimentation has been done except for trying the method out with eight students and refining the curriculum to its present state.

The Simulation of a Teaching Machine on the IBM 650[3]

Our choice of a general purpose digital computer for simulation of a teaching machine was guided by our desire for flexibility. This flexibility allows us to make changes in the teaching method without requiring that a new machine be built each time. The design of our machine is determined by the computer program. That is, the order and type of problems it presents to the student, the way it scores his answers, the method of knowledge of results, and how the presentation of material is modified if the student makes an error, are all embodied in the program of instructions to the computer. Any of these characteristics can be changed by merely changing the program of instructions.

The IBM 650 Inquiry Station is a typewriter and a console which is capable of transmitting typed information to the computer and receiving information from the computer. The student sits at the Inquiry Station. The program of instructions in the computer presents the problem to the student by way of the typewriter. The student, in turn, types his answer, which is transmitted to the computer for checking.

The program of instructions consists of six parts corresponding to the six steps involved in the teaching of binary arithmetic. The number of symbolic computer instructions for each of these parts varies from 200 for multiplication to 450 for division. The total number of instructions is approximately 2000. The computer uses between 4 and 30 instructions to check the students' responses, depending on what method is used. We could have stored the answers to all of the problems in the

---

[3]Mr. D. Middleton assisted in the programming.

program, and this method was used for the two sections
on binary to decimal conversion. Another method in
which the computer actually performs the arithmetic as
does the student was used for the Counting, Addition,
Subtraction, and Multiplication. For Division, the computer calculates part of the problem and checks the rest
with answers in storage. The choice of the methods for
each part was based on the ease of programming and the
efficient use of storage. Further details of the computer
program are available but are not presented here.

The psychological principles of efficient learning
that are built into the program of a simulated machine
are as follows. The student constructs his own response
in answering each problem. He must enter one unit or
bit of the response at a time. For example, in counting,
if the student is to answer with the number 1010, he enters
the first 1. The computer checks this number and if
wrong, types WRONG and modifies its program. Since
it takes only 50 milliseconds to check each unit, the
student can enter each unit of the answer as fast as possible until he is wrong. After the student completes
his answers to a problem, and is correct, the machine
presents the next problem. Thus, immediate knowledge
of a correct response consists of allowing the student
to continue until he makes a mistake.

One reason for scoring each unit of the response
is to indicate exactly where the error occurs for the
smallest unit of the response. As shown above, as soon
as one digit is wrong, the program types WRONG and
presents new material. This scoring of each unit of the
response also prohibits entering additional wrong numbers. For example, if all digits are correct, a new
problem is presented as soon as the last response is
made, even though the student might think another number
is to be entered. In Addition, if the answer should be 5
units long, as soon as the fifth unit is entered correctly,

the next problem is presented. We have not allowed the student to use an "end of answer symbol" in Addition, since we want to eliminate the possibility of entering an additional wrong number. However, in decimal to binary conversion, we score each unit but also require the student to both enter the binary number and indicate end of the answer. We felt this was necessary since in converting powers of 2 from decimal to binary, the number of zeros is the critical feature of the response to be learned.

The program allows for individual differences in skill level and rate of learning. If the student is making no errors, he is given an option to skip 2, 1, or no problems. After he enters his choice, the program is modified and presents a new problem dependent on his choice.

As mentioned previously, when the student makes an error, program prints WRONG, and presents another problem. The choice of this new problem depends on the number of errors the student has made in this part of the program. Counting, Addition, Subtraction, etc., are presented and scored as separate parts of the total program. If he has made fewer than X number of errors, the program presents a problem at the same difficulty level as the last problem he completed correctly. If he has made more than X errors he is presented a problem similar in difficulty to one of the first problems in that part of the program. The number of errors X which determines the program branching can be chosen on an a priori basis, or computed on the basis of each student's errors by a subprogram. In our program we chose X = 5, based on our experience with the teaching program.

The preceding discussion presents what we have programmed to date to simulate a teaching machine on the IBM 650, with the Inquiry Station Typewriter. We have no experimental results. Note that an experiment with this machine requires running one $\underline{S}$ in real time with the computer. Since the computer spends most of its time waiting for the student, suggestions for the utilization of this time are as follows: By multiplexing, the computer could present and score problems for several students who sat at different Inquiry Stations. Instructions to the student could be printed by the computer instead of given verbally as was done in our program. Also, the ordering of the problems by difficulty of concept was done heuristically in this program. The computer could be programmed to modify this order of presentation of problems by computing the difficulty of each problem as a function of students' performance.

In summary, we have simulated a binary arithmetic teaching machine on the IBM 650. Throughout the program we have employed several principles which are generally accepted as aiding efficient learning. The subject matter is presented and modified at a pace to suit the individual's skill level and rate of learning. The student constructs his own response, the machine scores each unit of the response and gives immediate knowledge of results.

References

1. Hilgard, E. R. Theories of Learning, New York: Appleton-Century-Crofts, Inc., 1956, Second Edition.

2. McCracken, D. D. Digital Computer Programming, London: John Wiley and Sons, Inc., 1957.

3. McGeoch, J. A. and Irion, A. L. The Psychol. of Human Learning, New York: Longmans, Green and Co., 1952, Second Edition.

4. Osgood, C. E. Method and Theory in Exper. Psychol., New York: Oxford University Press, 1953.

5. Pressey, S. L. Development and appraisals of devices
    providing immediate automatic scoring of objective
    tests and concomitant self-instruction, J. Psychol. ,
    1950, 29, 417-47.

6. Richards, R. K. Arithmetic Operations in Digital
    Computers, New York: D. Van Nostrand Co. , Inc. ,
    1955.

7. Skinner, B. F. The science of learning and the art of
    teaching. Harvard Educ. , Rev. , 1954, 24, No. 2,
    86-97,

8. Skinner, B. F. Teaching machines. Science, 1958,
    128, No. 3330, 969-977.

9. Wickens, D. D. and Meyer, D. R. Psychology,
    New York: The Dryden Press, Inc. , 1955.

12

Leslie J. Briggs

Hughes Aircraft Company

TEACHING MACHINES FOR
TRAINING OF MILITARY PERSONNEL
IN MAINTAINANCE OF
ELECTRONIC EQUIPMENT

One purpose of this paper is to describe briefly four teaching machines developed to promote more efficient learning, by Air Force trainees, of the knowledges and skills required in maintenance of electronic equipment. A second purpose is to point up some of the research questions for which answers are needed to guide further developments in this area.

The Apparent Nature of the Material to be Learned

Description of the overt behavior of an electronic technician performing his work in the field situation is not very difficult. He can easily be observed to look at dials, twist knobs, consult the field manual, replace faulty electronic units with good ones, etc. The motor responses by which the technician tests, adjusts, troubleshoots, and repairs the system and its units are quite evident. However, it is not equally apparent how he decides or is cued to do what he does, nor how he learned to do it. Existing descriptions of what he must learn during training and how it should be taught, taken together, sound much like the verbal reports of the blind men who "saw" the elephant. So we shall not burden the reader

The opinions expressed in this report are the author's; they do not necessarily reflect the opinions of the United States Air Force nor of Hughes Aircraft Company.

with another lengthy report of this sort. Research is
greatly needed first to establish, for these maintenance
jobs, the content of what should be taught. If this were
known, we could next proceed to develop the teaching
machines and other techniques by which the learning
could be achieved. However, it appears likely that much
of the progress on these two undertakings may go hand
in hand, in small steps.

Without venturing, then, into all of the details
of another blind man's description of the subject matter
the trainee presumably needs, briefly we may state the
following requirements, some of which recently have
been identified by Gagné and Bolles (Chap. II). The
technician does have to learn to find and to recognize
literally hundreds of objects and parts in the equipment.
Some of this learning is done by memory, and some by
learning how to use indexes and charts as guides. The
technician does have to follow many fixed sequences of
actions; some of the brief ones he performs by memory;
the more lengthy ones are performed with the aid of a
checklist. The technician does have to learn many concepts and rules which are used to decide when and how
to perform acts which are not or cannot be specified in
manuals for each occasion they may be needed. Related
to learning of concepts and rules is the need to understand the fundamental principles of the functioning of
electronic circuits. And somewhere between such general
principles of circuit function on one hand, and fixed
procedures of maintenance on the other, there appears
a need for an understanding of the general objectives of
the specific equipment in terms of "what it is trying to do."
This appears somewhat different in nature from the
ability to follow functional diagrams intended to depict
how the system does what it is trying to do. Additional
requirements also probably exist, depending upon the
specific job or the equipment, for: learning to make use
of simple formulae; to use hand tools; to make complex

judgments; to use general rules to guide the deductive thinking required in troubleshooting; to transpose readily from symbols to words to actual physical appearance of hundreds of objects, etc.

In the absence of the research needed to spell out the details of the above requirements, the writer offers the following preliminary hypotheses as to what should be taught and how this may be accomplished.

1. Many facts, locations, identifications, and rules could best be learned "in isolation" from the practice of the total motor sequences of job operation in which they are normally used. The problem is to identify these elements and to program them effectively into teaching machines. At least two attempts in this direction yielded encouraging results (5, 10).

2. Some brief fixed sequences need to be memorized and performed without reference to the manual. The problem is to find out whether these could best be memorized serially in the form of verbal statements and then practiced on the equipment, or whether they are best learned by direct practice on the equipment. One study tends to suggest that the first of these two procedures (5) may sometimes be most effective.

3. Lengthy procedures, composed of elements of performance like those items in categories 1 and 2 above, but cued by manuals or checklists, may need to be practiced in a real-life simulated situation in order to insure development of a rapid smoothly-running "consolidation" of performance of all the separate items into the total complex sequence.

4. Information concerning what the system is trying to do, and how it is trying to do it normally is imparted by lectures illustrated by reference to data flow diagrams.

This information appears to be needed for troubleshooting.
When this information is not available to the technician,
he is forced into trial-and-error procedures, or into
extremely laborious attempts to "figure out" the same
information from detailed circuit diagrams. It appears
conceivable that at least part of this requirement eventually could be met by programming of troubleshooting
trainers.

5. Troubleshooting is a skill which initially could not be
well taught by direct practice. Its component skills are
somewhat difficult to identify, but no doubt they are largely related to understanding equipment operation in terms
of schematic and data-flow diagrams, and in use of these
diagrams as the basis for logical deductions as to where
to perform measurements. All of the elements in items
1 and 4 above, may at times be a part of troubleshooting
skill. Also needed is the ability to understand the basis
and significance of observed wave forms and voltages.
After instruction in such "fundamental skill components, "
practice in a simulated or real life situation appears
advisable to apply rules governing the strategy of troubleshooting. At least one experiment yielded promising
results from the application of these assumptions about
troubleshooting (7).

Due to the large numbers of required procedural
sequences and troubleshooting problems, training cannot
and need not provide direct practice in all of them. If the
component fundamental skills and knowledge are properly
identified and learned, practice of small representative
samples of these maintenance procedures may be sufficient to promote transfer to the job situation when the
problems arise.

Some Maintenance Training Devices

As a result of the very general kind of hypothe-
sizing summarized above, two kinds of devices have been

developed. On one hand, we seek simple devices to establish efficient learning, whether by memorization or by concept formation, of the individual items or knowledge components of total maintenance procedures, probably learned "in isolation" from the context of the complete procedures themselves. On the other hand, we seek methods for providing, in the total procedural context, whatever practice is needed to "consolidate" the learned elements into the sequences of operations and problem solving situations which the job requires.

Two types of devices will be described, each directed toward achievement of one of the above requirements.

Multiple Choice Devices

For learning of many of the knowledge elements apart from the procedures in which they belong, and for "verbal pre-training" to memorize short maintenance sequences, two devices have been developed. Pictures and descriptions of these two devices are found elsewhere (3). Both devices employ a multiple-choice situation, and are referred to, respectively, as the Subject-Matter Trainer and the Card-Sort Device. [1]

The Subject-Matter Trainer. The device presents stimulus items (up to 20) in a fixed sequence. On a response panel are mounted the 20 choices, each of which is the correct answer to one of the stimulus items. For initial trials, the device shows the student the correct answers by means of signal lights opposite each answer. The student works at his own pace, leaving each right-answer

[1]These two devices were developed while the writer was employed by the Maintenance Laboratory of AFPTRC (ARDC), Lowry Air Force Base, Colorado. The devices are now located at the Aero-Medical Laboratory, WADC, Wright-Patterson Air Force Base. Patents pending.

light glowing as long as he wishes. On later trials, the
student first must make a response by pressing a switch
adjacent to an answer. If the choice is correct, the
signal light glows, and the student may go on to the next
item when he desires. If the answer is wrong, this is
indicated, but immediately after, the light glows next to
the correct answer, thus prompting the student, and
restricting him to one overt error. Other modes of
practice, selected by a master control knob, permit:
multiple errors; changes in the type of signals given;
automatic temporal pacing, and several other features,
including "scrambling" of the relative location of the
various response alternatives. A "test" mode also is
provided, with automatic scoring. Probability of overt
errors is thus, in general, under several types of experimental variation.

　　　　The Subject-Matter Trainer has been used in at
least four classroom or field situations, and in several
laboratory studies, with informative and encouraging results. The results of some of these try-outs were reported only in informal unpublished memoranda, and are
thus not available for reference. However, three published reports do exist. Two dealt with field use (5, 10),
and one with the relative effectiveness of the various
modes of use as investigated in a laboratory situation (9).

The Card-Sort Device. This device provides approximately
the same operating conditions as those of the Subject-
Matter Trainer, except that the stimulus item and either
two, three, or four alternate answers appear on cards,
one for each item. Up to 100 items may be presented in
a series. On this device, however, each card is sorted
into one of two retaining wells, depending upon the correctness or incorrectness of the student's first response
to the item (even though the second response on the first
exposure may be correct). Thus, on successive trials,
the "wrong" stacks of cards only may be presented until

none remains. If desired both decks can be used, and cards may be "shuffled" between trials if desired.

The writer has had no opportunity to conduct studies with this device, although it is possible that this may be done by others.

Procedural and Troubleshooting Trainers[2]

Just as complex "simulators" have been found useful in training of pilots and other operators of equipment, it is believed there may be a need for complex maintenance trainers, in order to practice total, realistic job tasks in a context sufficiently similar to the job situation to promote transfer. Such devices also would provide practice of the "elements" learned previously by multiple-choice and other devices and techniques. In part, the reason for considering this type of device is to achieve the stimulus similarity which may be needed between the training and the job situations. It also is possible, in maintenance procedures, that if one response made is essentially a cue or stimulus for the next response, the same similarity is needed on the response side.

For various reasons, the complex procedural aspect of maintenance was simulated in one device, and troubleshooting conditions were represented in another. The training characteristics of these two devices previously have been discussed (2, 6), as well as the general engineering design (11).

In the Procedural Trainer, the physical aspects

---

[2]These two devices were developed through the stage of engineering design by Hughes Aircraft Company, under Contract No. AF 41 (657) - 83, with ARDC. Plans for further research study and equipment development are now being made.

of the equipment and its functions are simulated;
automatically-programmed sequential instructions are
employed along with feedback signals, in order to provide the trainee automatic instruction in fixed sequences
of activities. In this simulated maintenance situation
written instructions, such as would be provided in a
field manual, are presented as stimulus materials.
While the trainee performs, the system "freezes" if an
error is made, and the source of the error and the
acceptable corrective action are indicated. Upon resump-
tion of correct procedure, the system "un-freezes," and
the next instruction is presented. Thus the device affords
guided practice in the manual accomplishment of complex,
fixed procedures, for which instructions in written form
would be available in the field situation. For appropriate
briefer sequences, memorization of the stimulus materials also is provided to afford learning to perform without
dependence upon the manual.

The Troubleshooting Trainer has the same simulated features as the procedural trainer, with means for
affording the trainee practice in making wise sequences
of checks while attempting to isolate a trouble. This
device, by the use of logic circuits, indicates after each
check whether it is a reasonable check, considering the
total series of preceding checks, and indicates the equipment area involved, and why.

Both of these complex trainers, it is to be noted,
employ performance guidance, performance feedback, and
performance recording. Both require correct performance
as a condition for the presentation of the next step in a
procedure. The nature, and if appropriate, the probable
reason, for errors is automatically given. Repeated practice to perfection may be required for a single task, or
the trainee may be permitted to proceed to the next
sequence after one correct performance. In the troubleshooting device, the rules and logic of procedure are

explained, and instruction is given in progressively
limiting the equipment area probably defective. The
effectiveness of each response is indicated in terms of
this successive progression in terms of following the
rules given.

A word may be said here concerning use of such
devices for performance measurement. Research and
practical use of such devices is enhanced by automatic
performance recording and analysis. In part, the usefulness of such data is dependent upon the degree of
similarity between performance on the device and performance on actual equipment. Previous research with
a simpler simulator found the device highly satisfactory
in this respect (1, 4). For scoring troubleshooting
performance, a composite of many criterion components
appears needed (7).

Further development and testing of such complex
trainers is needed before conclusions as to their usefulness may be made. Experimental models of such devices,
which can readily be modified in certain respects, would
be extremely useful in some of the research issues discussed below. At present, however, it is known that at
least one device, somewhat similar in some respects to
those discussed here, though with fewer automatic features,
proved to be useful (8).

The Need for Further Definition of the Learning Requirement and the Training Method

The preceding section presents our present
understanding of what needs to be learned and one
hypothesis as to how it might be taught to provide high
transfer to performance in the job situation. As indicated
above, many of these broad assumptions appear to be
supported by empirical results; some of these results
were obtained with the devices described in this report.

Nevertheless more analysis and research is needed in defining these issues in order to give further direction to teaching machine development. Some of the research needed appears to center about the following questions.

1. For lengthy fixed procedures, once the elements of physical locations, identification of objects, etc., are learned, what are the problems in translating the printed instruction in the manual into successful action? Do stimuli generalize across sensory modalities automatically? If not, is it more economical to practice on the equipment from the start, if the stimulus noted in the manual (visual) must be experienced on the equipment as auditory, tactile, or kinaesthetic?

2. When must the response made in training be highly similar to that required on the job? When is the R1 equivalent to S2?

3. For memorized sequences, in which the single steps could easily be learned "out of context" from the task, what is the most effective way of establishing the "linkages?" Does this vary according to the psychological homogeneity or heterogeneity of the task elements?

4. For memorized sequences in which: each end response is motor in nature; the stimuli are mixed (some received by several sensory modes, some are verbal recall, some require reading); and some steps require "mediating" responses and some do not, is practice of the total task as such more effective than dealing with the elements "in isolation?"

5. What factors do determine when verbal learning is effective preparation for maintenance tasks?

6. How can tasks be identified as to the amount of concept-using required and the results be translated into guidance for training?

7. When is it more economical for the trainee to learn
by rote, and when by understanding the situation and
improvising his own procedures?

8. How does the equipment design and characteristics of
the maintenance tasks relate to the need for understanding
of the electronic theory pertaining to the functioning of
the equipment? How does the needed degree of molarity
or molecularity of the understanding of equipment function vary among maintenance tasks? Similarly, how does
the molarity of learning theory needed to arrange training vary, if it does?

9. Does the fact that a task appears "complex" (i. e., may
require recall of facts, application of concepts, utilization
of stimuli and mediators of many sorts, memorization of
sequences, and several response modalities) mean that
there are several kinds of learning involved, and if so,
what does this mean for training?

10. When should training devices be "task-oriented, "
and when "element-oriented?"

11. How many training devices are needed? One for
each "kind of learning" involved? One for each "element"
of a task? One for each type of task? One for each job?
One for each S-R bond to be formed? What is the best
compromise when, psychologically, several appear desirable, but few can be afforded?

12. How can trainers be sound both on the grounds that
the learning has been "analyzed" and each behavior
"tailor-developed, " and still be practical in cost, training time, transfer, and practical success?

13. How can maintenance behavior be usefully "analyzed"
psychologically so that these data practically can be employed in synthesis for building successful trainers?

The writer contends that the eventual development of an adequate theory of teaching machines rests not only upon the progress of learning theory and programming techniques, but also upon progress in description of the kinds of learning for which teaching machines are needed and in applied experimentation in real-life training situations. No one teaching machine, it is argued, is likely to be successful for all learning situations.

Maintenance of electronic equipment and training for maintenance is the central point of discussion. Since performance of a complex job is the criterion performance sought, the discussion cannot be restricted to one "pure" type of learning, such as serial rote memorization or learning of verbal paired-associates. Efforts to describe the training needed touch upon some characteristics of performance in the job situation, some subject-matter identification, and hypotheses concerning the kind of training methods which appear to be needed.

Two types of teaching machines are briefly described. One type of device deals with learning of isolated verbal facts and concepts and with verbal memorization of brief sequences of procedures later to be performed through motor response made upon actual equipment. The second type of device, intended to teach complex procedures and troubleshooting in a simulated job-equipment situation, appears needed to "consolidate" or provide practice in linking together the elements of skill learned separately, and to enhance the probable degree of transfer to actual job performance. Studies are cited concerning field and laboratory experience with some of these devices, in terms of the subject-matter of training and the measurement of proficiency of the trainee.

An attempt is made to specify some of the research needed to throw light upon what needs to be learned; how such learning relates to job performance; and why present difficulties in dealing with both the subject-matter and the psychological aspects in the required learning need to be resolved. The question as to how to provide sufficient analysis of the material to use psychological knowledge of learning in devising trainers, while remaining realistic in terms of the training time, maintenance task-unit integrity, and job requirements, is raised as a problem needing intensive study.

References

1. Besnard, G. G. , and Briggs, L. J. Comparison of performance upon the E-4 Fire Control System simulator and upon operational equipment.   Lackland Air Force Base, Tex. : Air Force Personnel and Training Research Center, 1956. Development Report. (AFPTRC - TN - 56 - 47).

2. Briggs, L. J. Design of maintenance training equipment for fighter-interceptor fire control systems. Lowry Air Force Base, Colo. : Maintenance Laboratory, AFPTRC, August 1957. Technical Memorandum. (ML - TM - 57 - 16).

3. Briggs, L. J. Two self-instructional devices. Psychological Reports, 1958, 4, 671-676.

4. Briggs, L. J. , Besnard, G. G. , and Walker, E. S. An E-4 Fire Control System performance test: I. Functional description. Lowry Air Force Base, Colo. : Armament Systems Personnel Research Laboratory, AFPTRC, March 1955. Technical Memorandum. (ASPRL - TM - 55 - 8).

5. Briggs, L. J. and Besnard, G. G. Experimental procedures for increasing reinforced practice in training Air Force mechanics for an electronic system.   In G. Finch & F. Cameron (Eds.), Symposium on

Air Force human engineering, personnel, and training
research. Washington: Nat. Acad. Sci. , Nat. Res:
Council, Publication 455, 1956. pp. 48-58. (AFPTRC-
TN - 56 - 24, January 1956).

6. Briggs, L. J. , and Du Vall, W. E. Design of two fire
control system maintenance training devices. Lackland
Air Force Base, Tex. : Air Force Personnel and
Training Research Center, September 1957. Technical
Report. (AFPTRC - TR - 57 - 7). ASTIA Document
No. 134242).

7. Chalmers, E..L. , Jr. , Morrison, E. J. , Briggs, L. J. ,
and Pens, E. H. Evaluation of a method for teaching
troubleshooting techniques. Lowry Air Force Base,
Colo. : Maintenance Laboratory, AFPTRC, December
1957. Technical Memorandum. (ML - TM - 57 - 34).

8. French, R. S. Evaluation of a K-System trouble-
shooting trainer. In G. Finch and F. Cameron (Eds,),
Symposium on Air Force human engineering, personnel,
and training research. Washington: Nat. Acad. Sci. ,
Nat. Res. Council, Publication 455, 1956. pp. 160-165.
(AFPTRC - TN - 56 - 15, January 1956).

9. Irion, A. L. , and Briggs, L. J. Learning task and mode
of operation variables in use of the Subject-Matter
Trainer. Lackland Air Force Base, Tex. : Air Force
Personnel and Training Research Center, October 1957.
Technical Report. (AFPTRC - TR - 57 - 8).

10. Mayer, Sylvia R. , and Westfield, R. L. A field
tryout of a teaching machine for training in
SAGE operations. Bedford, Mass, : Operational
Applications Laboratory, Air Force Cambridge
Research Center, ARDC, October 1958 (OAL -
TM - 58 - 16).

11. Pens, E. H.   Explanation of the functional block
diagrams for two self-instructional fire control
system maintenance trainers.   Lowry Air Force
Base, Colo. : Maintenance Laboratory, AFPTRC,
December 1957.   Technical Memorandum.
(ML - TM - 57 - 17).

13

A. A. Lumsdaine

American Institute for Research

PARTIAL AND MORE COMPLETE
AUTOMATION OF TEACHING
IN GROUP AND INDIVIDUAL
LEARNING SITUATIONS

The connotation of the term "automation of teaching" in the title of this paper is meant to extend somewhat beyond that of "teaching machines." The notion of automated instruction could really include teaching by any instructor-saving contrivance, including instructional films as well as Skinner's machines (12) and certainly encompassing the self-scoring tests of Pressey and others (e. g. , 5, 10). Also included would be the non-machine programmed textbook or workbook combinations--"scrambled" or otherwise--that are described elsewhere in this symposium by Crowder (Chapter X) and by Homme and Glaser (Chapter IX).

Let us consider automated instructional methods to include any means, devices or materials, whereby teacher or tutoring functions are provided by wholly or partially automated sequences of instruction that are completely prepared in advance of use, and that are capable of instructing effectively when presented with minimal direct participation by a teacher. The kind of instructor function automated differs in different cases, and the degree of automation may be conceived to vary from slight to complete, being inverse to the extent to which the actions of a teacher, a monitor, or the student himself are required to govern the sequence of instruction or to score or record student behavior.

147

Of particular interest are those automated instructional methods that have two important properties. First, a great deal of active student response is required, providing explicit practice and testing of the major parts of what is to be learned. Second, some basis is provided for informing the student with minimal delay whether each response he makes is correct, leading him directly or indirectly to correction of his errors.

Automation of Group and Individual Instruction

These characteristics are found in individual tutoring or Socratic teaching, both with machine and human tutors. They are not found, of course, in the usual lecture nor in the semiautomated surrogate for the lecture represented by the conventional form of film, tape recorded lecture, or instructional TV presentation. However, they can be and have been achieved in varying degrees with certain special kinds of group-presented films, film strips and other forms of recorded instruction that provide for frequent interspersing of questions or practice segments and presentation. These can be especially effective when used with appropriate adjunctive materials on devices to facilitate the making and/or scoring of appropriate student responses.

Such automated group instructional techniques, using alternated presentation, question and response, have much in common with individual teaching machines. The latter differ primarily in the feature of more flexible pacing that readily adapts to differing rates of progress of which individual students are capable. Despite the unquestioned potential advantage of this individual-pacing feature, it is to be noted that some group-instruction techniques can offer many of the advantages of individual teaching machines (e. g. , controlled sequencing, prior programming, provision for active response, correction-feedback, etc.). Also, they may in some instances have

economic and other features that make them easier to
introduce into current educational situations. Finally,
research on variables that govern their effectiveness, of
which some examples are presented in this paper, can be
of direct relevance to the design of teaching machines
and teaching machine programs.

Evolution of Automated Group Instruction

For group instruction, we may think of lecture
presentation as a starting point and modal form. The
obviously most complete surrogate for the live lecture is
the filmed lecture or lecture-demonstration. However,
the use of films for educational purposes did not start
off with this concept of a teacher surrogate, of teacher
talking several-steps-removed to students via intermedia-
tion of camera, processing and projector. Rather, for
some years the prevailing concept was that of the film as
an adjunctive teaching aid, particularly for providing so-
called "enrichment" by supplying stimuli that teacher
and text could not readily supply. This was the concept
of "bringing the world to the classroom. "

Teaching films designed to convey more specific
instructional content began to appear in quantity during
the thirties, and burgeoned in the proliferation of so-
called training films, on nearly every conceivable topic,
that were produced by the Armed Forces during World
War II. Partly for reasons of traditionalism and partly
because many of these films were ill-equipped to stand
on their own feet as effective instruction, it continued to
be emphasized more or less piously, however that these
films were teaching aids, not instructor substitutes.
The idea of actually putting a complete course or course
unit on film or recording it on tape as the primary vehicle
of instruction emerged somewhat later. Only in very
recent years have we really implemented the possibilities
of full-fledged filmed courses, as exemplified by the

high school physics film courses made at TV Station
WQED by Professor Harvey White under sponsorship of
the Fund for the Advancement of Education.

One of the first attempts to provide a full course
unit in which the information-transmission function of
the teacher was provided entirely by recorded instruction
was made by Newman and Highland (9) as a project of the
Training Aids Research Laboratory of the former Air
Force Personnel and Training Research Center. This
project was reported in an Illinois newspaper in August,
1954 under the headline,

"MECHANICAL INSTRUCTORS? COULD BE . . !"

The article continued in part: "If mass mobilization came
tomorrow, there would be an extreme shortage of skilled
technical instructors. In this case, could tape recordings
be used for presenting technical material to Air Force
trainees? . . . In an experiment conducted by Drs. Newman
and Highland at Keesler Air Force Base, several classes
were taught a five-day course in Principle of Radio by
highly qualified instructors. Other classes were taught
the same course by tape recordings and either a workbook or slides. When students. . .were given a written
examination covering the course, the grades of students
who were taught using the tape-recorded lectures were
about as high as those of the students taught by the
instructors. "

At about the same time, an attempt was made
by the same laboratory to mechanize the giving of training lectures to B-47 jet bomber technicians by recording
lecture demonstrations on films. These filmed lectures
were shown by test data to approximate closely the
effectiveness of the live lectures. It should be added
that the filmed (i. e. , automated) lectures offered very
real economic advantages, particularly for training of

small, widely scattered groups of technicians. Also, they had the advantage that they could be scheduled flexibly and presented immediately before their content was to be applied. Their use could thus avoid the very large decrements in recall that were found to take place during the frequent lapse of several weeks between presentation of a "live" lecture and its application on the job (11).

Active Student Response

This kind of partially automated group instruction by filmed lecture may help offset instructor shortages, but it still retains the essentially one-way, passive-reception character of any lecture instruction since, as such, it makes no effective provision for frequent active student response and feedback. Thus it might substitute for but not improve substantially on conventional class instruction by lecture methods. This fact is, of course, really a general criticism of the lecture as a basic method of instruction, not a special one of its automated reproduction. It highlights the notion that it is especially for their active-response and feedback properties, rather than solely for the standardizable reduplication characteristic of automation as such, that teaching machines and some of their counterparts should be of primary interest to educators.

However, it is quite possible to incorporate active-response features in a combined recording, film and workbook package designed for group instruction. An example is provided by a package course developed at the Air Force's former Training Aids Research Laboratory. This course was designed for teaching English as a foreign language to aviation personnel in MDAP or NATO countries where no experienced instructors could be counted on. In this case, each section of tape or film instruction presented to a class was designed

to elicit active practice through workbook exercises used
in close conjunction with the recorded and film-presented
instruction. The materials for this six-week course are
shown in Figure 1. Persons who have been impressed
with the magnitude of the task of preparing material
needed to program a course for teaching machines may
be interested in the quite large amount of materials required for this instructorless, semi-automated film and
tape course. These materials were prepared by four
or five persons in about nine months. They were almost
completely "programmed," in the sense in which that
term is in use at this symposium, and they incorporated
some of the same principles (e. g., progression through
easy stages to more and more complex forms of syntactic
behavior) that have been applied more recently to programming of materials for individual teaching machine
or programmed-book presentation.

The main point to be made here is that there
are many kinds of possibilities for applying mechanized
or partially automated techniques in teaching, and that
some of the same ideas that have given impetus to the
development of individual teaching machines may readily
find fruitful application in group-instruction situations.
This may possibly occur, in the case of many schools,
well prior to the time when the applications of individual
machine tutoring are regarded as economically feasible
and culturally acceptable.

Some Experiments on Factors in Automated Instruction

Of the properties of group-instruction devices
that involve active response and feedback, several may
be singled out for comment because they are of recurrent
general interest in discussions of programmed teaching,
and because, in addition, some experimental evidence
concerning them is available. This evidence bears on
their status as design factors worth paying an economic

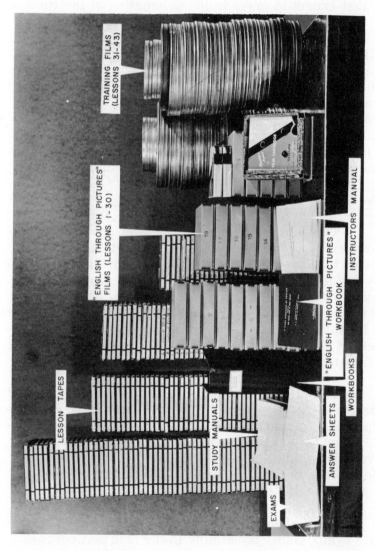

Figure 1. Materials for six-week "instructorless" course for teaching English to foreign personnel, using active-practice exercises with film and tape presentation.

or psychological price for, in the design compromises
one must expect to make in the automating of instruction.

The variables or design factors in the studies to
be cited are: (a) the role of active response or feedback
in contributing to learning under favorable and unfavorable
conditions; (b) the motivation and practice components of
this active responding; (c) the results of increasing the
percentage of correct responses through "response
guidance" or use of "prompts"; and (d) the effect of variation in size or difficulty of instructional "steps" or
segments.

Active Response with Feedback

The earliest and most widely cited of these
experiments was performed during World War II and was
reported by Hovland, Lumsdaine and Sheffield (3) in 1949.
Many readers will be familiar with it. A film was used
to teach the military phonetic alphabet, Able for A,
Baker for B, and so forth, plus some related information.
Two forms of the film were compared in order to study
the effect of using active review, or so-called "audience
participation."

The difference between the two forms was solely
in the review sequences. The control film used a standard
or "passive" form of review, in which letters were presented along with their phonetic equivalents. In the
active review, the letters only were presented, and the
audience members were instructed to try to call out the
correct equivalents for each letter in turn.

The "prompts" to adopt the terminology common
in this symposium, lay simply in the fact that correct
equivalents had been recently presented, providing a
basis for their being emitted during the review. Feedback-
correction and/or further "prompts" were provided by

the fact that the group had to <u>call out</u> each response. Since someone almost always gave a recognizably correct answer, correction-prompts were almost always thereby provided.

Figure 2 shows the advantage of the active-response or so-called participation procedures, as

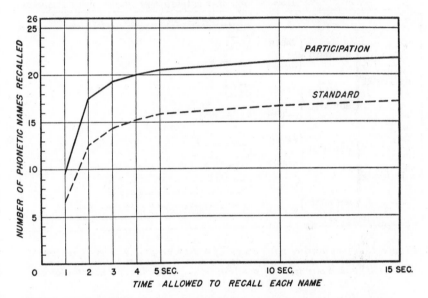

Figure 2. Advantage of "participation" or active-practice as compared with standard (passive review) versions of a film for teaching phonetic alphabet equivalents, in terms of average number of phonetic names correctly recalled within designated periods of time per name. Reproduced from Hovland, Lumsdaine, & Sheffield (3).

found by Hovland, Lumsdaine and Sheffield. These surveys show the comparison between the active and passive groups at various criteria of recall-promptness in oral tests given at the end of the training. The asymptote for the active group could be, and was in later experimentation (8), raised to near-perfect by increasing the amount of repetition of the response sequences. Figure 3 shows the fact, of interest in determining the importance of the

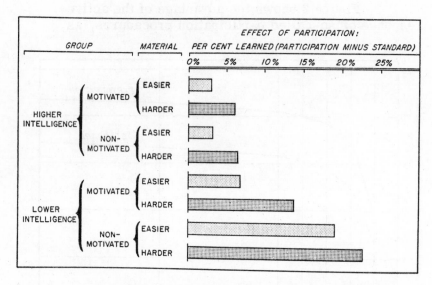

Figure 3. Comparative advantage of active-response form of review as affected by difficulty of material and the intelligence and motivation of the learners. Reproduced from Hovland, Lumsdaine, & Sheffield (3).

active-response and feedback procedure, that its advantages were least when least needed and most when most needed--i. e. , greatest for less motivated, slower students in learning the more difficult material, and least for brighter, highly motivated students in learning the easier material.

The fact that the task to be mastered by students in these two studies was the acquisition of "rote"

paired-associate responses may not be overly discour-
aging to those who, like the author, believe that useful
predictions for more complex learning can often be based
on the same assumptions about associative processes
that seem useful in accounting for the acquisition of
simpler associations. Regardless of theoretical predilec-
tion, the results may also seem not without interest to
educators who are impressed with the enormous fund of
basically paired-associate response acquisition required
in mastering, for example, the lexical elements of foreign languages, medical terminology, or the nomenclature
of almost any technical subject matter--paired-associate
prerequisites that are indispensable to later conceptual
manipulation involving the acquired terms.

     A number of additional experiments have been
done in the past eight years or so that extend our knowledge of factors important in the use of frequent active-
recitation or practice sequences to modify the passive-
reception drawbacks of the customary forms of film or
lecture. Some of these studies have recently been
reviewed by Allen (1), though many of them are not
currently available outside of government reports with
limited circulation. Most of them were concerned with
acquisition of response patterns in more complex contexts than simple rote identification of isolated paired
associates. It seems worthwhile to cite here the results
of three of these studies to illustrate their bearing on
factors which may enter into the design of machine-
presented or other programmed learning materials.

     The first of these studies was reported by
Maccoby and Michael in 1953 (6). The subject matter
was of a substantive verbal type, dealing with defense
against atomic attack. As in the phonetic alphabet study,
active student response was provided at intervals between sections of film exposition by the insertion of
question and answer sequences. Responses were written

rather than oral, and feedback, following student response, was therefore given by announcement of the correct answer to each question rather than by pickup from an oral class chorusing.

The focus of the study was on three aspects of the use of Socratic review sequences--(1) motivational as against practice effects; (2) overt as against covert responding, and (3) the importance of feedback in the form of response-correction. The dominant role of the practice factor is shown by comparing the results for passive or no-participation group with those for active-response groups that answered questions after each

Average Percent of Correct Answers for Participation Groups on Practiced Items and on Non-Practiced Items, Compared with Average Performance of Non-Participation Groups.

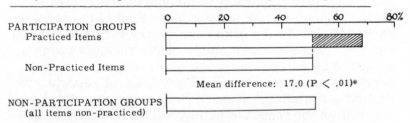

Figure 4. Practice versus motivation components of an active-review procedure. Data are from a study by Michael and Maccoby (6).

segment of exposition. The results for the latter were
analyzed separately for test questions that were directly
covered by the practice questions and those that were
not. The results (Figure 4) showed that the gains from
active response were wholly attributable to specific
practice effects rather than to motivational benefits ac-
cruing to items not specifically practiced. (It should be
pointed out that the items tested were discrete factual
items, so we are not concerned here with generalization
effects on the non-practiced materials.) In a later repli-
cation of this experiment by S. Levine, using less interesting subject matter, some motivational effects were
revealed in terms of gains on non-practiced items; but
even here the dominant effects were those of direct
practice.

Other comparisons in the Michael and Maccoby
experiment showed that the largest single factor in determining the efficacy of the active response procedure was
the provision of feedback correction through giving the
correct answer after each question had been responded
to by the students. In this particular experiment, finally,
covert or subvocal response was about as effective as
overt written response.

In a study by Kimble and Wulff (4), a combination of film strips and workbooks was used to teach the
reading of logarithmic scales commonly employed in the
slide rule and similar analog computing devices. Kimble
and Wulff were interested in what is basically the "crutch"
or "prompt" question--that is, the amount of guidance
to be provided as students proceeded through a practice
schedule that alternated short practice exercises with
short segments of exposition or demonstration. Automated
exposition was presented to groups of subjects in a
classroom situation by use of a film strip accompanied
by a synchronized tape recording. Students did practice
exercises in workbooks in which slide rule scales or

portions of them were reproduced. Responses consisted of giving the numerical value of a marked scale reading, or conversely, finding a specified value on the scale. All groups were given the same exposition and the same amount of practice. The major experimental variable was the use of prompts or response guidance.

Figure 5 shows one of the several ways in which prompts were provided. Asked to locate 0.62, the

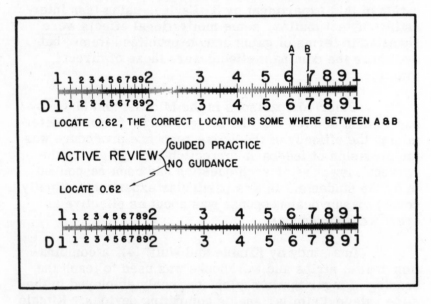

Figure 5. "Guided" and "unguided" forms of practice exercise used with a film for teaching reading of slide-rule scales. Used in a study by Kimble & Wulff (4).

guided-practice group was provided with a constraint which limited the possible responses but without speci-fying exactly the correct response. The no-guidance group was allowed to make more errors by withholding such prompts. It should be made clear that in all cases the students had already been told how to do a similar exercise, and that further instruction was given as follow-up after each exercise.

The results showed a clear margin of superiority for the "babied" or prompted group. This group, the one that was given prompts on most exercises, did better on a later test not only on the items used in practice but also in transferring to other similar items. The margin for superiority was greater on hard items than for easy ones, and was greatest where the prompts had been chosen to help the student avoid certain types of errors which preliminary work had shown were the ones most commonly made.

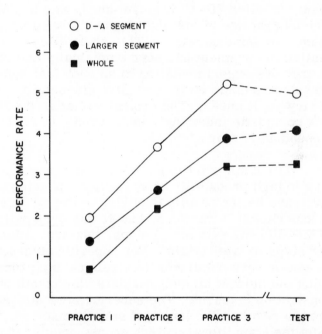

Figure 6.   Comparative performance on practice and final test for a mechanical assembly task when the length of filmed-demonstration segments shown between periods was valid. Reproduced from Maccoby and Sheffield (7).

The last experiment to be cited was reported
by Maccoby and Sheffield (7). Like the preceding experiment, it manipulated conditions that affect the
probability of a correct response during training. Here,
however, the tasks to be learned were sequential procedures. These were presented in a filmed demonstration
several times, with practice following each demonstration.
The variation that affected probability of correct response
was the "size of step, " or length of sequence demonstrated
before each practice period. Results for one of the tasks
studied are shown in Figure 6. The poorest performance,
both during practice and on later tests, was when the
entire task was demonstrated, then practiced. The best
performance was when demonstration of only a short
segment, labelled "D-A" segment here, was followed
at once by practice of just that segment, before the next
segment was demonstrated. (This short "Demonstration-
Assimilation" segment had been empirically determined
from previous experimentation to be such that some 75%
of the subjects could do it perfectly, given sufficient time,
after viewing it once.) The ordinal values in the figure
were a composite index that took account, in effect, of
both speed and errors.

The main point to be noted is that small steps,
leading to high probability of students responding correctly, gave better results than larger steps. In a related experiment it was found that it was even better to
start the students with small steps, then transition to
larger steps in later trials. For superior students, the
best results were obtained with a self-pacing procedure
in which the student himself regulated the length of the
demonstration segment. The superior students, when
allowed to regulate the length of step themselves, tended
to adopt the transitional pattern spontaneously, starting
with short easy steps on the first trial but ending with
whole practice by their last trial.

Figure 7. Sketch showing use of an "automated" film-demonstration device for teaching complex procedural tasks.

Figure 8. Prototype model of an automatic sound-film projector developed by the Air Force Personnel and Training Research Center. Pre-threaded film loop is completely contained in magazine inserted at the right of the projector, thus providing an automatic projector device.

The application of these and relating findings in the teaching of shop and laboratory procedures to technicians and scientists would be facilitated by general availability of a demonstrational teaching machine in the form of an automatic film projector, of which a prototype is shown in Figure 7. As shown in Figure 8, such a device can be stopped at any point desired, permitting the technician to check his work against a picture that remains on the screen and, for most tasks, brings the percentage of correct response for each step up to virtually 100%. This error-free practice means that the technician can learn while he does useful work, gradually transitioning to longer and longer steps as he learns.

The illustrative results cited above illustrate the feasibility and desirability of systematic experimental manipulation of the conditions of programmed instruction incorporating sequences of presentation and recitation, question-and-answer, or demonstration and imitative practice. Obviously, they represent only one approach and only a modest beginning toward the experimental analysis of variables in practice conditions that affect the design of devices and of programs, for automated individual or group instruction, employing alternated presentation and guided, checked, student response.

References

1. Allen, W. H. Research on film use: Student partici-
    pation. Audio-visual Communication Review, 1957,
    5, 423-450.

2. Hoehn, A. J. , & Lumsdaine, A. A. Design and use
    of job aids for communicating technical information.
    Air Force Personnel and Training Research Center,
    Technical Report AFPTRC-TR-58-7, January, 1958.
    (ASTIA Document No. AD 152-109)

3. Hovland, C. I., Lumsdaine, A. A., & Sheffield, F. D.
    Experiments on Mass Communication. Princeton:
    Princeton University Press, 1949.

4. Kimble, G. A., & Wulff, J. J. The effect of "response
    guidance" on the value of audience participation in
    training film instruction. USAF Human Factors
    Operations Research Laboratories, Washington, D. C.,
    1953. (HFORL Report No. 34)

5. Little, J. K. Results of use of machines for testing
    and for drill, upon learning in educational psychology.
    J. exp. Educ., 1934, 3, 45-49.

6. Michael, D. N., & Maccoby, N. Factors influencing
    verbal learning from films under conditions of
    audience participation. J. exp. Psychol., 1953,
    46, 411-418.

7. Maccoby, N., & Sheffield, F. D. Theory and experi-
    mental research on the teaching of complex sequential
    procedures by alternate demonstration and practice.
    Paper presented at the Air Force - National Research
    Council Science Symposium on Personnel, Training,
    and Human Engineering, 1956.

8. May, M. A., & Lumsdaine, A. A. Learning from films.
    New Haven: Yale University Press, 1958.

9. Newman, S. E., & Highland, R. W. The effectiveness of
    four instructional methods at different stages of a course.
    Air Force Personnel and Training Research Center, Air
    Research and Development Command, Technical Report
    AFPTRC-TN-56-88, June 1956.

10. Pressey, S. L. Development and appraisal of de-
    vices providing immediate automatic scoring of
    objective tests and concomitant self-instructions.
    J. Psychol., 1950, 29, 417-447.

11. Shettel, H. H. , Faison, E. J. , Roshal, S. M. , & Lumsdaine, A. A. An experimental comparison of "live" and filmed lectures employing mobile training devices. Audio-visual Communication Review, 1956, 4 (No. 3), 216-22.

12. Skinner, B. F. Teaching machines. Science, 1958, 128, 969-977.

14

David Zeaman

University of Connecticut

SKINNER'S THEORY OF

TEACHING MACHINES

One of the differences between the natural and the social sciences is that in the natural sciences, each succeeding generation stands on the shoulders of those that have gone before, while in the social sciences, each generation steps in the faces of its predecessors.

Whether psychology is a natural science or an unnatural one may be a question, but given a practical psychological problem of training devices to solve, there is no question at all that we have a choice of two strategies here, the shoulder or the face.

If it is the shoulder, where should the constructor and the programmer of human training devices look in the scientific literature of psychology for experimental data relevant to his task?

Any answer to this question implies a theory of training devices. It is in this loose but yet important sense that the word theory is here used.

Skinner has a theory, if I read him rightly, and it says the appropriate reference class of experiments, the appropriate experimental paradigm, for construction and programming teaching machines is that of free operant conditioning. Others, in particular those using the memory drum, are held to be inappropriate.

167

Skinner's resolution of the shoulder-face question is, happily, the shoulder, but the shoulders are too ivy-league-ish--too narrow.

It is the counter-thesis of this talk, that existing teaching machines (and those likely soon to be built) represent complex admixtures of at least three basic experimental paradigms, free operant, controlled operant, and classical conditioning, and that of these, the free operant may be the least pertinent. Furthermore, of all the commonly used apparatuses for experimental study of learning that one which most closely resembles one of Skinner's teaching machines, (the Write-in Model) is the memory drum.

Since there is something less than universal agreement on classification of learning paradigms, let me ask for a temporary convention in the use of the words "controlled operant, free operant, and classical conditioning."

All three refer to experimental arrangements of observable variables that a machine can handle. The common elements of all three include two stimulus events S_1 and S_2, occurring in that order, and at least two responses arbitrarily designated as correct and incorrect.

By "controlled operant" or "discrete trial operant" is meant those experiments incorporating the following acquisition features: (keeping the Graham-Gagné Runway experiments in mind will help you here).

The acquisition trial begins with the presentation of a stimulus situation S_1 which lasts until the subject makes a correct response - R. One and <u>only</u> one correct response R occurs per trial because the correct response terminates S_1. It also brings S_2, which in this case is a reinforcing stimulus. S_2 does <u>not</u> elicit R.

The timing arrangements are partially subject controlled, partially experimenter. The time interval between S_1 and S_2 is subject controlled since S_2 is contingent upon R, but the intertrial interval, that is the S_2-S_1 interval is usually under the experimenter's control.

Acquisition is measured by S-R latency or the conditional probability of R given S_1.

Illustrative apparatuses for controlled operant conditioning include the runway, Miller-Mowrer Shuttle Box, Retractible Bar Skinner Box, the Single-door Lashley Jumping Stand, and also if correction technique is used, the Simple T-Maze, Discrimination Boxes and the Two-door Jumping Stand.

In the free operant or ordinary Skinner box situation, similar features are present with some exceptions. The initial stimulus situation S_1 is of prolonged duration, allowing many correct responses to occur, each one reinforced during continuous acquisition by the contingent reinforcing stimulus S_2. This of course permits a rate measure to be taken.

Both the free and controlled operant paradigms, then, display an SRS sequence, with the second S contingent upon R. The big difference lies in the number of correct responses allowed per trial, only one in the controlled operant (since the correct response eliminated S_1 as well as bringing S_2), but <u>many</u> correct responses in the free operant.

What about timing differences? Is one self-paced and the other not? If one accepts Estes' analysis of the free operant, the animal turns S_1 on and off by himself, even though the experimenter leaves it on. Each reinforcing stimulus S_2 turns over the S_1 and the subject gets a fresh look at S_1. In this analysis, the free operant is self-paced, in the sense that the subject controls the intertrial interval, the time between S_2 and S_1.

This is to be contrasted with the controlled operant in which the subject waits for the experimenter to turn on S_1. It is not completely self-paced.

It is important to note here that if you accept this analysis and regard the free operant as self-paced, it is only so when the S_1's remain the same.

If the experimenter has a number of different S_1's to be connected to a number of different correct responses, free operant techniques can be used, but then it is no longer completely self-paced. The experimenter changes the problem. The inter-problem interval is not subject controlled, and it is this interval that we are usually interested in with teaching machines.

Now finally to the classical conditioning paradigm. The previous two paradigms were SRS sequences with a contingency. This one is an SSR sequence with no contingency. To fulfill the paradigm, the first stimulus S_1 must not elicit R as strongly as you would wish, whereas the second stimulus S_2 must elicit R, the correct response.

This is a highly operational, non-theoretical specification of the classical conditioning paradigm. It is not asserted that S_2 be an innate elicitor of R, nor even a strong stimulus. Whether such a paradigm always provides the necessary or sufficient conditions for learning is an empirical question not easily resolved, given the existing literature. It is, however, a paradigm that can be used in construction of training devices, and it looks operationally at least to be different from free and controlled operant conditioning, in not having a contingent S_2 and in requiring S_2 to elicit the correct response.

In the matter of timing, classical conditioning resembles the controlled operant in that the experimenter controls the inter-trial interval, (the S_2, S_1 gap) but classical conditioning differs from both free and controlled operants in also giving control over the S_1 - S_2 interval to the experimenter.

With these three paradigms specified in this way, let us take a look at three pieces of apparatus, a memory drum set up for paired associates, Skinner's Write-in Model teaching machine and Skinner's Arithmetic machine.

First the paired associates experiment. On the first trial around, there is ordinarily no anticipation. The subject sees the S_1 syllable and reads the correct associate. This fits the classical conditioning paradigm. It is an SSR sequence, no contingency, and all stimulus intervals under control of the experimenter.

On the second and subsequent trials, the possibility of operant conditioning enters. If the subject correctly anticipates the associate, he is reinforced by the match of his anticipated answer and the forced answer. Since this matching or knowledge of correct results, is contingent upon a correct anticipation, elements of a controlled operant are present.

If the subject gives the wrong response, the contingent reinforcement is not present, and the trial resembles an extinction trial of a controlled operant. The trial ends, of course, with a classical conditioning feature, a forcing of the correct response, elicited by the appearance of the associate.

If no overt response is given at all, the trial becomes a simple classical conditioning trial again.

Thus there are three kinds of trials possible with a paired associates machine, a simple classical trial, a controlled operant acquisition trial with a terminal classical feature, or a controlled operant extinction trial with a terminal classical feature. The timing of these trials is almost exclusively that of a classical conditioning, however both the S1 - S2 interval and the S2 - S1 interval are experimenter controlled. To my knowledge there are no animal experiments with trials at all like these, although I believe they might be arranged.

Consider now, Skinner's Write-in Model learning machine. It presents a written question or an incompleted sentence or paragraph in an aperture, and then waits for the subject to write in his answer or completion. Following this the subject operates the machine to present the correct written answer to be compared with his own. The next problem appears when the subject indicates to the machine that he is ready.

We analyze the machine in the terms used before. As with the memory drum there are three kinds of trials, depending upon whether the subject makes no response, makes the correct response, or makes an incorrect response.

If no response is made, the trial looks like a classical conditioning paradigm or SSR. The question stimulus S1 is presented. Then the answer stimulus follows, and elicits the answer response. No contingency, just a forced response like classical conditioning.

If the correct response is made, an instrumental or operant feature emerges. The correct answer given in anticipation of S2 is reinforced by a matching of the correct results. This reinforcement is of course contingent, and makes the trial resemble the free or controlled operant. But since there is only one correct

response made, this aspect of the trial looks most like
the controlled operant.

If an <u>incorrect</u> response is made, the contingent
matching <u>reinforcement</u> is absent and we have elements
of a controlled operant extinction trial. The trial is
terminated however with the forced response characteristic
of the classical procedure.

The high similarity of these three kinds of trials
with those of the paired associates memory drum experiment is obvious.   Yet there is some difference.
A difference in timing. With the usual paired associates
procedure, all stimulus intervals are <u>experimenter</u>
controlled. With the Write-in Model, in contrast, the
S_1 - S_2 interval is <u>subject</u> controlled (that is, the subject
can give himself as much time as he wants before presenting S_2) and the interproblem interval is also subject
controlled. It is indeed a self-paced device.

The subject's control of the timing of the S_2
stimulus is by no means new: it is a property of free
and controlled operant procedures in general, but the
subject's control of the interproblem interval is relatively novel. It is <u>not</u> found in either the usual controlled
operant experiment, or in the usual free operant, nor of
course, in classical conditioning. Some recent experiments on the role of observing responses in animal
discrimination have incorporated an analogous type of
paradigm. Wyckoff had pigeons turning on their own
discriminative stimuli by stepping on a treadle. His
work should be relevant to this machine. And other work
may be relevant too.

Since there have been so many memory drum
experiments done, and since it is no engineering trick
at all to convert the usual memory drum to an entirely
self-paced apparatus, like Skinner's Write-in Model,

I would be surprised if a literature survey failed to turn up any self-paced paired associates data. Of course when a subject riffles through a deck of flash cards at his own time, the paradigm for this primitive machine is the same as that of Skinner's Write-in Model.

The last device to be inspected is a modification of one of Skinner's devices which we have also constructed and called the "Arithmachine." It presents visual material and allows the subject to make any of a large number of numerical responses, one of which is correct. The response is the movement of sliders and the turning of a crank. If the sliders have been positioned correctly, each slider position representing a number, the turning of the crank will bring reinforcement and the next problem.

The analysis. This machine operation looks much more like the controlled operant procedure than does the Write-in Model. The S_1 or question is presented, a response is waited for, and a contingency set up. If the response is correct, the subject is rewarded by the complete turning of the crank and whatever other reinforcing signals the experimenter wants. There are no forced responses of a classical nature at the end of the trial. The correct response not only brings reinforcement, it eliminates S_1, the question stimulus, thus allowing only one correct response per trial, the hallmark of the controlled operant.

Timing is not completely self-paced. The S_1 - S_2 interval is subject controlled, but the interproblem interval is not. The problems come in massed sequence. As soon as the subject finds out that he has been right on the last problem, the new one stares up at him.

Strength of acquisition is inferred with this apparatus from latency or probability of response, as it is for the other machines mentioned. Free rate of operant response, in the presence of a prolonged S_1 is not taken here, nor is it a measure taken for any teaching machine that I know of.

This machine, in summary, embodies all of the elements of the controlled operant, and the literature on this kind of experiment may therefore be relevant.

In final summary, the original question is re-asked, where should the constructor and programmer of human training devices look in the scientific literature of psychology for experimental data relevant to his task Any answer to this question implies a theory of training devices. If Skinner's theory says that the literature on free operant is most relevant, this paper proposes the counter theory that the literature of controlled operant and classical conditioning is also relevant but more so.

If Skinner's theory says that memory drum experiments provide an inappropriate model for construction of training devices, this paper proposes the counter theory that no other experimental device or procedure more closely resembles Skinner's Write-in Machine than a common memory drum paradigm.

Old Ebbinghaus's shoulders may not be ivy-league, but we ought to stand on them anyway.

PARADIGMS

A) <u>CONTROLLED</u> <u>OPERANT</u>

Trial 1   Trial 2

S_1 R S_2 S_1 R S_2

Subject   Experimenter
Controlled   Controlled

B) <u>FREE</u> <u>OPERANT</u>

Trial 1   Trial 2

S_1 R S_2 R S_2 R S_2 S_1 R S_2 R S_2 R S_2

Subject   Experimenter
Controlled   Controlled

C) <u>CLASSICAL</u> <u>CONDITIONING</u>

Trial 1   Trial 2

S_1 S_2 R S_1 S_2 R

Experimenter   Experimenter
Controlled   Controlled

15

Howard H. Kendler

New York University

TEACHING MACHINES

AND PSYCHOLOGICAL THEORY

When I accepted the invitation to comment on teaching machines, I was under the impression that the audience would be small but nevertheless would contain a wide spectrum of opinions. I had the premonition that some psychologist, probably from the Midwest, would criticize the whole "teaching machine movement" because it was not based upon a solid foundation of clearly defined theoretical principles. I was absolutely certain that enthusiastic supporters of teaching machines would be present and extoll the virtues of teaching machines while ignoring, or failing to understand, the comments of the theoretically-oriented psychologist. I expected, perhaps even hoped, that some dignified, elderly humanist would voice fears concerning the threat teaching machines posed not only to the dignity of teachers, but also to the cultural standards of our entire society.

I decided to rebut the assumptions upon which these three positions were based. When I finished I was surprised to discover that my rebuttal contained a kernel of agreement with each of these three views. Perhaps, I thought, I would play the role of peacemaker at this conference.

I soon learned that my expectations were wrong. The audience was large and their attitudes ranged from a passionate devotion to a sympathetic acceptance of the teaching machine. Obviously I could not play the role of peacemaker, because except for a few remarks (especially those of Professor Zeaman), peace reigned supreme. After hearing the initial papers with their reports of various teaching machine programs, I became uncomfortably convinced that my prepared statements were inappropriate for this conference. After hearing all the papers I persuaded myself that my paper, although inappropriate, was not irrelevant. With this sort of self-encouragement, I decided to present essentially the paper I had prepared which, for reasons better known to others, was placed at the end of the program.

Professor Skinner in a recent article (10) and a number of lectures has extolled the virtues of teaching machines. Psychologists can feel proud (a sensation that is for them all too rare) that one of their kind has taken it upon himself to develop an educational technique which promises so much in solving not only some of our pressing educational problems, but also improving the educational process itself. The importance of immediate reinforcement--or feedback--is obvious to every student of learning. The teaching machine can be the most efficient exploiter of this basic educational mechanism. The teaching machine is also an efficient device to shape a student's behavior so that he can gradually proceed from simple, concrete ideas to complex, abstract ones without being retarded or advanced too rapidly by his fellow students.

One cannot--at least I cannot--argue against the eminent reasonableness of Professor Skinner's enthusiastic support of the idea of adopting the teaching machine as an integral part of our educational system. His arguments are so sensible that I am forced to conclude that major resistance to teaching machines must stem from emotional bias or misconceptions about how they are to be used.

Now that I have unequivocally expressed positive
attitudes toward teaching machines, I can safely air some
reservations without my remarks being interpreted as
being critical of the teaching machines per se. In short,
my remarks are concerned not with the use of teaching
machines but instead with the problem of increasing their
usefulness.

There is always a tendency to lump together
ideas that have a common origin. Although the recent
development of the teaching machine is obviously an
outgrowth of Skinner's operant conditioning programs, it
would be useful to isolate, for a moment at least, the
teaching machine as an educational instrument from
Skinner's atheoretical, ultrapositivistic systematic position. It is my belief that if we come to grips with
problems that properly belong to theories of learning
and problem solving, that we may increase the effectiveness of the teaching machine. One can go very far in
controlling behavior with an atheoretical, ultrapositivistic
orientation. Yet even finer control, I believe, will be
achieved after dealing with basic theoretical problems
in the science of behavior.

The area of transfer of training has been minimized, if not ignored, by most researchers in the
"teaching machine" area. There are several facets to
this problem that must be considered in sound educational
programming.

I need only point to my own research program,
with whose specific facts I will not burden you. This
program has been interested in discovering how the
learning of one concept influences the learning of another
concept. Another way of expressing this interest is to
say that I am concerned with how individuals utilize their
concepts in a new situation. For example, college students can accomplish a reversal shift more rapidly than

a nonreversal shift (4). Rats, in contrast, find it much
easier to execute a nonreversal shift (3). More recently
it has been found (5) that kindergarten children, as a
group, showed no significant difference between the speed
in which they accomplished a reversal and nonreversal
shift. At first glance they appear to fall halfway between
the behavior of rats and college students. However, when
this group was broken down into fast and slow learners
on the initial discrimination, it was found that (a) for
slow learners (as for rats) reversal shift was slower
than nonreversal, and (b) for fast learners (as for college
students) reversal was faster than non-reversal. Obviously, then, the learning of a particular concept does
not insure that it will be transferred in only one way.
Performance, in short, is not a perfect indicator of
transfer. An S-R mediational theory has been postulated
to account for these and other findings. A mediational
assumption is not new. Several psychologists in past
generations have postulated that in some situations behavior is not directly linked to environmental stimuli,
but instead is mediated by implicit responses that function as cues for subsequent implicit or overt behavior.

Skinner himself emphasizes the mediational
process (e. g. , 9). The fact that both Skinner and S-R
mediational theorists (e. g. , 8) postulate mediational
events (implicit stimuli and responses) does not mean
that they are all indulging in the same sort of behavioral
analysis. Skinner is proclaiming that implicit S-R events
function as do observable S-R relationships. In contrast
is the approach of the S-R mediational theorists who
accept as a model of "symbolic" behavior the theoretical
principles that have been formulated to account for S-R
relationships in simple learning situations. Whereas
Skinner is essentially legislating the laws of symbolic
behavior, the S-R mediational theorists are proposing
an extension of a theoretical system to a new set of
phenomena. It is more than likely that this attempt at

extension, if successful, will require the postulation of
new theoretical constructs and/or new theoretical relationships. As I see it, an arbitrary declaration that
mediational events obey the laws of observable S-R
correlations alters a reasonable hypothetical proposition
into a factual statement and thereby avoids answering
basic questions by refusing to ask them.

Let us return to mediational processes. Experimental results (5) seem to indicate that problem
solving is intimately related to the ability of organisms
to generate appropriate response produced cues. These
cues mediate the transfer from one situation to another
with the amount and kind of transfer, depending on the
implicit responses of the subject. Are these findings,
and their interpretation, inconsistent with the implications of Professor Skinner's following remarks?

"The role of the teacher may well be changed,
for machine instruction will affect several traditional
practices. Students may continue to be grouped in
'grades' or 'classes,' but it will be possible for each to
proceed at his own level, advancing as rapidly as he
can. The other kind of 'grade' will also change its
meaning. In traditional practice a C means that a
student has a smattering of a whole course. But if machine instruction assures mastery at every stage, a
grade will be useful only in showing how far a student
has gone. C might mean that he is halfway through a
course. Given enough time he will be able to get an A;
and since A is no longer a motivating device, this is
fair enough." (10, p. 976).

Professor Skinner seems to be ignoring the
problem of transfer. One need only refer to the
classical work on overlearning (6) to show that
performance may not mirror how much has been
learned.

I would be very surprised if we were unable to discover large differences in the ability of subjects to transfer what they have learned after completing the same "teaching machine program." Differences in transfer could arise from a number of sources (e. g. , differences in the implicit mediating responses, genetic differences, amount of learning). The simple point that I am making is that we should not initially accept the completion of a programmed course as the final criterion of learning. We should be persistent in asking questions as to what is being transferred from a particular learning experience. Unless we ask this important question no answer will be forthcoming.

A better conception of the psychology of transfer and symbolic processes must be achieved to do full justice to teaching machines. And by a better conception I do not simply mean how responses can function as cues. What must be understood is how simple verbal responses develop into abstract ones and these in turn result in still higher abstractions. How does the cue function of abstractions change as their level of abstraction increases What must also be understood is how different responses merge together to produce novel forms of intellectual behavior. Although novelty is obviously a function of past experience, we are still very unclear about the mediational processes that generate novel behavior.

Increased knowledge about the psychology of transfer and symbolic processes would enable us to program courses that will generate the kind and amount of transfer we desire. I might also add if we knew a bit more about transfer we could have more confidence that good programming would become a scientific technology instead of remaining an art.

My next point is also closely related to the problem of transfer, but is far removed from programming specific courses. Jenkins and Russell (2) at the University of Minnesota have been doing yeoman's service in understanding the psychological structure of our language. The results of word-association tests given over a span of 23 years suggest that we as a society are becoming more homogeneous in our verbal habits. The percentage of students at the University of Minnesota giving the most popular responses increased from an average in 1929 of 29% of the 100 Kent-Rosanoff words to an average of 38% in 1952. Perhaps this change reflects the greater impact on our daily lives of such mass media as television and radio. Or perhaps our school systems have become more standardized. But whatever the reason, assuming the facts are correct (there are obviously many possible confounding factors such as the smaller percentage of the population going to college in 1929), we are faced with a serious threat to our national scientific creativity if Guilford (1) and others (7) are correct that word-association originality facilitates problem solving. In contrast the word-association norms of the French and Germans have been shown to be less uniform. Another threat exists in the finding (2) that our language habits are becoming less abstract and more concrete. Perhaps this trend toward uniformity and concreteness is responsible for what appears to be a tendency for the great scientific discoveries of recent decades (except in psychology, of course) to be made by foreigners.

I do not wish to burden teaching machines with this global problem. I feel that it would be strategic for the researchers in the field of teaching machines to wear blinders for the time being (a bit of advice that seems to be accepted somewhat too enthusiastically). The basic problem now is to design technically proficient machines and discover their capabilities in limited educational situations. But ultimately the implications of a mass, standardized educational program (and I think teaching machines will lead to this) will have to be faced. It is particularly important that any large-scale educational program constantly check on the transferability of what is being learned. There is no inherent reason why an educational program transmitted via teaching machines would discourage the development of "creative" thinkers. We should not assume, however, that they would automatically be produced.

Let me repeat the gist of my remarks. There is no psychological principle of which I am aware that would oppose the use of teaching machines. Conversely, there are several principles that would suggest that the teaching machine would be an effective and efficient educational tool. Ultimately we have to develop better theories of behavior, particularly those of transfer and symbolic processes, in order to make the best use of teaching machines. Although it might be unstrategic to consider these theoretical problems immediately, I think it would be more unstrategic to deny their existence.

References

1. Guilford, J. P. Creativity. Amer. Psychol., 1950, 5, 444-454.

2. Jenkins, J. J. and Russell, W. A. A comparative study of word association norms. Technical Report No. 22, ONR Contract No. 8 onr-66216, University of Minnesota, 1958.

3. Kelleher, R. T. Discrimination as a function of reversal and nonreversal shifts. J. exp. Psychol., 1956, 51, 379-384.

4. Kendler, H. H. and D'Amato, M. F. A comparison of reversal shifts and nonreversal shifts in human concept formation behavior. J. exp. Psychol., 1955, 49, 165-174.

5. Kendler, T. S. and Kendler, H. H. Reversal and nonreversal shifts in kindergarten children (submitted to J. exp. Psychol., 1958).

6. Krueger, W. C. F. The effect of overlearning on retention. J, exp. Psychol., 1929, 12, 71-78.

7. Maltzman, I., Brooks, L. O., Bogartz, W., and Summers, S. S. The facilitation of problem solving by prior exposure to uncommon responses. J. exp. Psychol., 1958, 56, 399-406.

8. Osgood, C. E. Method and Theory in Experimental Psychology. New York: Oxford, 1953.

9. Skinner, B. F. Verbal Behavior. New York: Appleton-Century-Crofts, 1957.

10. Skinner, B. F. Teaching machines. Science, 1958, 128, 969-977.

16

S. L. Pressey

Ohio State University

CERTAIN MAJOR PSYCHO-EDUCATIONAL

ISSUES APPEARING IN THE

CONFERENCE ON TEACHING MACHINES

Related Previous Work

As background for a conference concerened with
means for more effective learning in such diverse fields
as Air Force pilot training, grade school arithmetic and
spelling, and college courses in psychology, it was
appropriate that in advance a review (Chap. II) be sent
to the participants summarizing relevant previous research bearing on this total topic. But is is startling to
find all the research (and also the relevant practical
know-how) in education bearing on this problem omitted
from consideration with the sweeping statement on the
first page that "educators, who work with practical learning situations, have not done the systematic, controlled
type of study that is needed to reveal general principles
of learning efficiency."

Rather, it would seem that a great variety of
relevant careful investigation had been done in education,
and in educational and industrial psychology. Thus a
brief search turned up the following: a demonstration
that arithmetic-readiness could be substantially increased
by sundry uses of number in the kindergarten, the findings
indicating something as to the ways children's number
concepts develop and possibilities of so preparing them
for machine teaching in arithmetic (6); indications that a
child's personality type influenced the effect on his

187

achievement of praise or blame and so perhaps of success
or mistakes on a teaching machine (15); evidence that the
teacher's understanding of each pupil as a person measur-
ably increased the amount each learned (9); evidence that
college students who were helped in correcting each other's
papers in a writing laboratory made more progress than
other students in a composition class where the papers
were corrected by the instructor (8). These were all
little studies. They were not put in terms of current
learning theory--were in a different universe of discourse.
But each was of "a systematic controlled type" with
reference to its topic. Each would seem to have some
relevance to the topic of this conference: surely readiness, personality-type, and what might be called the
social psychology of the classroom are all factors
affecting learning, worth psychological consideration--
and important to keep in mind in considering both the
potentialities and the possible limitations of mechanical
devices in teaching.

        Gagné and Bolles rightly stressed the impor-
tance of appraising the effectiveness of learning in terms
of outcomes not only in the learning situation but also in
"subsequent performance in a job situation." But they
seem unaware of the many careful investigations centering on just this point, in education and applied psychology.
In a volume published 15 years ago (10, p. 618ff.) a
chapter titled "Outcomes of Schooling: Applicational
Transfer" summarized research then in print on a variety
of topics such as on the value of safety education as
shown by reduction in accident rate, of a health education program as indicated by gains in weight of under-
nourished children, of a course in agricultural education
as evidenced by increases in yield of corn per acre on
the farms of those attending. Elaborate investigations
regarding values and possible faults of "progressive"
versus more conventional secondary schools have compared the later careers of the students as to proportion

going to college and success there both academically
and in student affairs.

Indeed, educational research taking account of
"performance in a job situation" well illustrates that
the reviewers should have considered it. So in school
safety education, investigators found where and under
what circumstances accidents did occur; no need to
stress accident-prevention where accidents never hap-
pened. Simply reading about safety in a textbook was
not enough; hazards were viewed, and safe procedures
practiced. Safety was made a topic in various subjects
as in arithmetic in handling accident data, and in science
in estimating automobile stopping distance at various
speeds. Posters tried to make the pupils "safety conscious"
and membership in safety councils to give prestige to
being careful rather than venturesome. Only at certain
points and in certain ways would it be likely that "teaching
machines" could help in such a program; and how would
need to be discovered by research such as mentioned
above, taking account of the total complexity of methods
and sought outcomes.

Moreover, such research might also contribute
to theory. Many applied psychologists regard most current learning theory somewhat as most theorists regard
Guthrie's conditioning; it is speciously neat, not coming
to grips with important complex problems. Hilgard has
declared (4, p. 461) that "there are probably a number of
different kinds of learning . . . . It is quite probable
that these different kinds of learning follow different laws."
Conceivably some of the very complex learnings mentioned in the previous paragraphs are different in kind
from the learnings from which most learning theory has
been derived--or at least so much more complex as to
follow somewhat different laws. Surely it would be un-
fortunate if current theories so dominated research
regarding teaching devices that such possibilities were

precluded from emerging. The writer would argue that
cooperation with educators and applied psychologists was
necessary for best work on the present applied problem,
and also elucidation of theory relative thereto. In his
introductory statement regarding the conference, Galanter
mentions the possible profitableness of "another conference after a few years. " Perhaps before that meeting
another review might well be prepared, by representatives
of these last groups, summarizing both investigations
and theories they think most relevant.

Ways of Using Teaching Machines

Self-instructional devices may be used as one
of several features, in a larger plan of instruction.
Little's 1934 paper (7) may well be cited. His is believed
the first systematic appraisal of such machines; in experimental design and adequacy of controls and data this
research of more than twenty-five years ago seems still
to stand as superior to anything recently reported--yet
his work seems overlooked in all recent bibliographies
and surveys of the field. Little's procedures were made
part of the regular routine, in certain sections of a 5-hour
required beginning course in educational psychology including laboratory exercises, informal class discussions,
and round-table discussions in groups of five, taught
each quarter in six or more sections each of about 30
students. About twice a week the experimental sections
began the work of the next two or three days by taking a
30-item true-false test on that material, each student
using a simple little machine on which he indicated "true"
by pressing the first key and "false" by pressing the
second; the next question was not turned up until the right
key was pressed, and a cumulative count of tries showed
in a "score" window. Each student whose score showed
that he had made an error then set his machine back to
zero (a very simple task) and went through the test again,
continuing until no error was made. Control sections

took the same tests but by the usual method of marking
them and then turning them in; test sheets were returned
the next day with errors checked and a count shown, and
then briefly discussed. Instructors were rotated and
like precautions taken. The basic experimental variable
was thus immediate as compared to delayed feedback.
All sections were given the same mid-terms and final
examinations, consisting of both multiple-choice and
essay questions. On these, the teaching machine cases
did markedly better than cases in the control sections
paired with them as to scores on an entrance test of
general ability and a pre-test at the beginning of the
course. In two other projects, groups of superior students omitted most or even all class meetings, the
course being covered under the guidance of self-
instructional tests, following most items of which were
page references or other cues for remedial study (1, 5).

Even this last procedure was essentially less
sweeping, however, than the bold and stimulating ventures of Skinner and his associates, which seem to make
programmed self-instructional material not simply an
addition to but almost a replacement of other instructional
methods and matter. Certain issues here seem to need
consideration not so much in criticism as in an effort
to free the method from certain limitations its theory
seems to put upon it.

The theory calls for short easy steps so that
almost every pupil may take them without stumbling,
errors being kept minimal. And the programming is
done a priori--somewhat oddly, for empirical-minded
psychologists. But investigation has shown most young-
sters who begin a subject already have some knowledge
of it, and pick up much incidentally as they proceed;
also, they commonly make only certain mistakes, and
these for determinable causes. Over-conscientious
schools have been shown to waste time teaching children

what they already know or will pick up for themselves, and trying to prevent unlikely errors. Might the present detailed programming be similarly over-meticulous, but become both briefer and more incisively effective, if account were taken of such investigations?

Moreover, may these common errors often need identification, with explication of their causes? In learning complex meaningful material, may several trials before success be educative? Might multiple-choice questions involving common misconceptions need identification as such, or considerations elucidative toward the best answer, all carefully planned for instructional rather than measuring purposes, be desirable? Wrong alternatives need not be like blind alleys in a rat-maze, but instead like cues, helping an inquiring mind delimit an idea. Though not here conclusive, it seems nevertheless of interest that Little's students who made most practice errors made most gains. A self-instructional device used with meaningful multiple-choice questions markedly reduced mistakes (14); so used in a college course, it increased the number of right answers on the final examination not only to the same questions thrice repeated, but also to questions on related topics (11, pp. 429-40). In short, there was spread or transfer. Conceivably for meaningful matter in a context, multiple-choice questions planned for use with a self-instructional device, and understood by the student as an aid for his learning, may have a greater effectiveness for that purpose than theoretical considerations might suggest. The stylized flat sameness of much current programmed material might then be relieved, with gains for certain purposes as dealing with common errors.

For the superior student especially, short-step very easy detailed programming might seem questionable. In reading he will probably skim a page for major ideas somewhat as he looks at a picture, in which if asked he will note that there are three trees and a house and so on, but may then perceive the picture less as a whole. And so it might be with programmed reading. Or consider the Ford Foundation's early admission students (3), 42% of whom skipped both junior and senior high school years, but 73% of whom were above average in academic record in college, and some 30% of whom in their college sophomore year scored on the Graduate Record Examination above the average first-year graduate student. To a programmer, is it not a bit disconcerting that some students can take such great leaps over two whole high school years (and a possible great pile of programmed matter) without evidence of academic injury but perhaps even gain? And suppose when a college sophomore, one of these students had entered a programmed course in psychology; would he have been expected to go through all the detail? Or would the independent study laboratory (5) mentioned earlier have been better, in which each student quickly skimmed an assignment, took a brief multiple-choice test on it covering main points and difficult issues using a self-instructional device, quickly checked back on items missed using the page reference following each question, discussed issues with other students or the laboratory assistant if he wished, then took a duplicate test to check himself out? The students thus covered the course in a short time, scored well on the final examination, and reported they had gained in self-confidence and ability to work independently. In these last respects, what might the effects of detailed programming be?

From these considerations, programming would seem to emerge as of great promise especially for certain kinds of material and certain purposes, but needing coordination with research on student needs, knowledge, and errors. And may there be danger that learning be made too much something one attempts in a booth alone with a machine and enmeshing programmed matter; most effective learning may rather be (as suggested early in this discussion) a varied lively challenging experience with frequent interplay of minds. Anyhow more widely useable and feasible now, and more flexible, would seem to be such procedures as used by Little and in the independent study laboratory, the self-instructional tests being aids to, rather than replacement of, present instructional methods and matter, stimulating rather than taking the place of discussion, giving cues for remedial study, and yielding scores helpful to both students and instructor.

Types of Devices

At least if the above conclusion is correct, now most needed may be something like a "chemo-card"--on which marks in "right" spaces at once change color but in "wrong" spaces do not--a device found successful ten years ago, but rejected by the Navy Office of Research on the ground that the cheap fountain pens involved would be too often stolen by trainees! Answer sheets responding selectively to pencil marking appear possible--and any such simple immediate feed-back scheme of exceedingly wide possible usefulness. Briggs' card-sort apparatus with selective review (2) seems the most versatile mechanism, Skinner's write-in devices most appropriate for some learnings but less where the task is to recognize or discriminate. Schools in the future may well use a variety of devices, each best for certain purposes. There are here many fascinating problems of ingenuity and coordination with psycho-educational findings regarding learning. Practicality may be crucial; the writer has found himself not continuing in his own classes the procedures that were successful there as experiments, but requiring much stuff and trouble! In retrospect, it seems odd that a conference expressly on "teaching machines" included no systematic discussion of such mechanisms.

Research Design: Need for Manifold Precautions,
and Early Appraising Experimentation

It is a commonplace of educational research that
first trials even of bad ideas usually come out well, because only teachers interested in them first try them,
and pupils like the novelty and the special attention. Almost any reasonable method involving pupil activity and
adjustment to individual differences will show gains.
Over 30 years ago it was reported that first grade children
teaching themselves to read, using clever materials
centering on a word-picture dictionary, gained more in
5 months than the average class in 2 years (13).

Appraisals should of course take account of
delayed as well as more immediate recall, and of transfer as shown by more adequate understanding of related
matter. There should also be testing or other appraisal
to determine (for example) what programming in a science
course may do to skill with apparatus in the laboratory
or readiness in identification of specimens on a botany
field trip. Evidence should especially be sought that
the learning is not narrowly verbal. There must be no
repetition of Horace Mann's experience of a century ago
in a geography class, which glibly answered questions
about various geographical features, but was entirely
unaware that these existed in that neighborhood, and was
unable to point them out. What are the effects on amount
and nature of class discussion? Does the special type
of reading involved in programming affect reading ability?
Are there (as was mentioned earlier) any effects on
know-how in working independently? Of course if possible there should be checks on "subsequent performance"
in a job situation. Occasionally something of this sort
can be done relatively easily; thus after a school hygiene
class considering desirable food choice, an unannounced
record was kept of the luncheons these students picked
in the school cafeteria. And since this is a practical

problem, there must be records of money, time, and trouble costs.

All these considerations argue for trial as early as possible, in regular classes with various teachers and the total complex of school or college life. Large college classes taught in many sections have many merits for this purpose. Control and experimental groups must give full consideration to the issues mentioned in the two previous paragraphs.

One little-mentioned advantage of a good self-instructional device is that it facilitates research. With enough materials and several sections of a large course available, it may be possible to gather useful data even in one day, process it the next, and so very rapidly get some helpful information on a variety of questions; e. g. desirable difficulty of questions, comparative value of different forms and arrangements of material, and so on (11, pp. 425-9). Sometimes the results may be very disillusioning. The writer found that one of his most promising layouts for self-instruction actually brought a bit less learning than the same total amount of time spent by the students simply in ordinary study. But a basic fact of life, for the applied scientist, should be kept always in mind: it is not enough that in the experimental situation the proposed new methods work well. They must do so in the average situation where they are to be used and with average people there; and they must there be sufficiently better than the methods and materials these same people have been using, that a change-over is both warranted and feasible. Early and frequent "acid tests" will guide the experimentation in this direction. They may prevent long and expensive ventures later found ineffective or at least impractical. They may also bring out alternative ideas which might otherwise not have been thought of.

References

1. Briggs, L. J., Intensive classes for superior students. J. of Educ. Psychol., 1947, 38, 207-215.

2. Briggs, L. J., Two self-instructional devices, Psychological Reports, 1958, 4, 617-676.

3. Fund for the Advancement of Education, They Went to College Early, New York; The Fund, 655 Madison Avenue, New York 21, New York.

4. Hilgard, E. R., Theories of Learning (second edition), New York: Appleton-Century-Crofts, 1956.

5. Jensen, B. T., An independent-study laboratory using self-scoring tests, J. of Educational Research, 1949, 43, 134-137.

6. Koenker, R. H., Arithmetic readiness at the kindergarten level, J. of Educ. Research, 1948, 42, 218-223.

7. Little, J. K., Results of use of machines for testing and for drill, upon learning in educational psychology, J. of Experimental Education, 1934, 3, 45-49.

8. Maize, R. C., Two methods of teaching English composition to retarded college freshmen, J. of Educ. Psychol., 1954, 45, 22-27.

9. Ojemann, R. H. and Wilkinson, F. R., The effect on pupil growth of an increase in teachers' understanding of pupil behavior, J. of Exper. Educ., 1939, 8, 143-147.

10. Pressey, S. L. and Robinson, F. P., Psychology and the New Education, New York: Harpers, 1944.

11. Pressey, S. L., Development and appraisal of
     devices providing immediate and automatic scoring
     of objective tests, and concommitant self-
     instruction, J. of Psychology, 1950, 29, 417-447.

12. Skinner, B. F., Teaching Machines, Science, 1958,
     128, 969-977.

13. Smith, Nila B., An experiment to determine the
     effectiveness of practice tests in teaching begin-
     ning reading, J. of Educ. Research, 1923, 7,
     213-228.

14. Stephens, A. L., Certain special factors involved
     in the law of effect, Abstracts of Doctoral
     Dissertations No. 64, The Ohio State University
     Press, 1953, pp. 505-511.

15. Thompson, G. G. and Hunnicutt, C. W., The effect
     of praise or blame on the work achievement of
     "introverts" and "extroverts, " J. of Educ. Psychol.
     1944, 35, 257-266.

Randall Library – UNCW

LB1029.A85 G3
Galanter / Automatic teaching; the state of the ar

NXWW

3049001861773